Miracles in Pinafores & Bluejeans

Ardeth Greene Kapp

Miracles in Pinafores & Bluejeans

Deseret Book Company
Salt Lake City, Utah
1977

Library of Congress Cataloging in Publication Data

   Kapp, Ardeth Greene, 1931–
   Miracles in pinafores and bluejeans
   Includes index.
   SUMMARY: A woman shares the experiences of herself
and others which exemplify the principles of living a
spiritually enriched life.
   1. Kapp, Ardeth Greene, 1931–   2. Mormons
and Mormonism in Utah—Biography. [1. Kapp, Ardeth
Green, 1931–   2. Mormons and Mormonism—
Biography   3. Christian life]   I. Title
BX8695.K35A35   289.3,3[B]   [92]
77–4268
ISBN 0–87747–644–6

To the many young women who have provided
the inspiration for these stories and to
those who will read them—some in pinafores,
and some in bluejeans.

Contents

Preface

I believe miracles are constant-
ly in the making, but often they go unnoticed because they
come in bits and pieces, here and there, and we fail to put
them together by removing the time and space that obscures
their reality. While hungering for evidence of a good life, we
may dismiss many precious gems that, if savored and held in
reserve, would at a later time fit together and then, like a
beautiful mosaic, become the very possession we so much
desire. I have found that seemingly unimportant events
linked together at a later time with other seemingly common
events become evidence of eternal principles on which faith is
built.

These true stories from the lives of young women that I
have chosen to share with you are those I have happened to
witness; they are not unlike those that may be yours each day.
My intent is to share true principles of obedience, sacrifice,
self-discipline, charity, faith, love, and determination that
can be repeated over and over again through the personal
experiences of you, the reader.

That these true and eternal principles might become
more evident as you develop an increased awareness and appreciation for the common, precious experiences of each day
is my desire. To this end I dedicate this book, with humble
gratitude for all those who, by their lives, have provided rich
and beautiful experiences in my life.

Acknowledgments

I am deeply grateful to my husband, Heber, for his constant expressions of confidence and encouragement and for his willingness to ease my work load by his pleasant and continuous support.

To my mother and my father, my brother and sisters and their families, I give thanks for contributing to a rich environment that has over the years revealed beauty in common things and miracles in every day.

I am grateful also to Eleanor Knowles, for her encouragement and expert editorial work; to Lowell Durham, Jr., for his professional assistance; and to Michael Clane Graves, Julie Fuhriman and Warren Luch for their excellence in the visual portrayal of the message of this book.

Chapter One

Between Here and There

*A*ll her other dolls had been lined up with care and placed aside, but at the close of the day, when all was quiet, there clutched in the bend of a fat little elbow was Sweetie Pie. Sweetie Pie had all the hair worn off the back of her head, one eye was missing, and one arm was almost detached. Yet there she was, tucked protectively under the arm of little three-year-old Shelley.

Standing in the twilight with the last rays of sun filtering through the shades, I looked long and thoughtfully at the quiet little girl now at rest from her play. Almost reverently I rearranged the covers as I bent down to feel both her warmth and that of Sweetie Pie. At that moment I thought I was witnessing the beginning of a miracle, and I marveled at the beauty of what I saw.

When does the preparation really begin? When do mighty souls become great mothers? What of the space between here and there? When is the season for gathering, acquiring, and developing? What of those attributes, skills, characteristics, and spiritual promptings that all become a part of the greatness? When do all the qualities of motherhood—the myriads of bits and pieces and combinations of beauty—come together? When does the divine kaleidoscope take final form and shape, so that no matter which way it turns or which parts are exposed, there is a new and different design, a pattern to enrich those exposed to its beauty, a spiritual reservoir from which all members of the family may one day partake? Surely Sweetie Pie had some place in the marvelous beginning of this preparation.

As I left Shelley tightly holding her treasure, I continued to ponder about the space between here and there. As a possible bridge for the gap, I thought about another little girl, Shirley, who some years before had been a little blonde in pigtails and bluejeans, with knuckles well calloused as evidence of her much-envied accomplishments. Shirley could outplay any boy or girl in the school in a game of marbles. She could draw a circle in the dirt, place her marbles along with the others in the center, and, with carefully selected taw and her knuckle buried in the dirt, aim with such precision that marbles flew in all directions beyond the ring. Her chapped and dirty knuckles were of little concern—except, that is, to her mother, who had such hopes of Shirley's hands mastering the piano keyboard or at least learning to play the hymns.

In time, like fruit gradually ripening in the summer sun, the maturing took place until one day Shirley came home excited, yet with some concern. She had been invited to a party! As if for the first time, she looked down and seemed to discover her faded blue jeans. Then she examined her hands, slowly turning them from front to back. Finally, with hope in her eyes, she anxiously exclaimed, "Look at my hands! What can I do about them? You've got to help me."

The scriptures tell us, "To every thing there is a season, and a time to every purpose under the heaven." (Ecclesiastes 3:1.) The time for marbles gradually slipped away, and in time Shirley's hands no longer bore evidence of her many coveted victories. Other victories were in the making.

It was on a Sunday afternoon several months later that Shirley, having been taught to keep the Sabbath day holy, walked to the dinner table with the big family Bible and interrupted the after-dinner conversation by taking a firm stand and announcing, "Dad, I can't find anywhere where it says, 'Thou shalt not ride thy bicycle on Sunday.' "

The space from here to there lessens when a free, determined spirit begins to search the scriptures to find answers to important questions.

Seasons came and went, and one day, when all the world seemed wide open to one prepared to step up and take what it served, Shirley announced, "I want to help the world turn, and I want to help it turn sharply. I want to make a mark in life."

With enough successes already to give her considerable confidence, her goals could be lofty. As she spoke of far-away places and exotic endeavors, her father posed a simple question with a not so simple answer. "Shirley," he said, "why don't you become great like your grandmother?"

Like a bird interrupted in flight, she excitedly asked, "What did she do?"

In a somewhat reflective tone, with thoughts of one gone for some years now, he replied, "She kept a beautiful home and raised a fine family."

The counsel was so brief, yet it seemed to weigh heavily. Aren't the skills to be a good homemaker just second nature, like breathing out and breathing in? Don't they just come with age and time and season?

Often during the following years her father's counsel would come to mind for Shirley at the most unexpected times, such as during a psychology class at college, or when she was organizing the election campaign for a student body candidate. It would come during a piano recital or when she was camping or learning first aid. It would seem logical when she was preparing for a Spiritual Living lesson, but why right in the middle of an economics class dealing with the gross national product? Why in the middle of a heated discussion with a roommate about the budget and the laundry? And especially why during general household responsibilities?

There were times of decision for Shirley, such as the decision that would have resulted in her forfeiting the lead in a play because of Sunday rehearsals. The decision-making was made easier when the schedule was changed to accommodate her needs. But while she dreamed of the lights and the stage, she could still hear the faint echo of what might one day be the command performance spoken of by her father.

Her experiences reached far and wide, as precious days seemed almost too packed with life. She must drink it all in, she thought—at least a sip from many wells, and hopefully more from some. From here to there seemed not so far now, for many experiences over the years had contributed to that rich and colorful kaleidoscope that was now hers to claim, for

3

she found the man of her choice. With her marriage date approaching, she reflected once again from a new point of view on the admonition to become great like her grandmother. "She kept a beautiful home and was prepared."

Was Shirley prepared? Had those precious preparation years that now seemed so fleeting been adequate to lay a careful foundation for a beautiful home? Only time would tell.

That was fourteen years ago—a good testing period, especially to anyone who visits in her home and observes the fruits of her labors. The Spirit of the Lord is there, and eight happy children. Shirley is a gifted and noble companion to her husband, the new stake president. They have a fine family and a beautiful home.

Those precious preparation years so vital, so urgently needed, had not been misused nor too soon interrupted. They had merely been handled carefully, awaiting the proper season. From here to there—so quick in passing.

Again I returned to Shelley's bedside, her covers now kicked off to provide more freedom of movement. Sweetie Pie was still clutched tightly in her arm. Surely this was another great and noble mother in the making.

Chapter Two

"You Are the
Only Friend I Have"

I had a memorable experience when I first began teaching in the public school system. A little girl came into my class at the beginning of the year and her first comment was, "I don't want to be in your class." I felt rather insecure myself, and I thought, *I don't blame you. I don't want to be here either.*

"Where would you like to be, Connie?" I asked. She replied, "I want to be in Miss Bingham's class." And I thought of Miss Bingham, who was better looking and younger and more fun, and who had the prettiest room in the school.

But Connie had been assigned to my room, so I tried to work with her and to understand her. Each time she would say "I don't want to come to class," I gave her all the attention I could. I practiced all the principles of good teaching I knew. I extended love, I tried to communicate, and I attempted to find out what her interests were. We started building a relationship, and I was beginning to feel pretty good.

Then one day we were having a creative writing assignment in an English class, and Connie came up to me and said, "Here's my assignment. I would like you to read it."

I said, "Just put it in the file, and I'll read it after class."

"No," she said, "please read it right now."

So I picked up the paper and read: "I hate you. You are ugly. You wear funny shoes." Well, she was right about that. When you're a teacher and have a lot of running around to do, you don't always wear the nicest-looking shoes.

I returned to the paper and continued: "You have hair on your arms." And I remember looking down and feeling shocked and thinking, *Sure enough.* She had also written, "And your hair's a mess." I had been out to recess with the children, and it probably was.

My first reaction was, *You little rascal, after all I've done for you! What kind of gratitude is that?* Then something in my heart said, "Wait. Try to understand this child." So with the help of an inner spirit, I looked at the paper and said, "Connie, your writing is really improving. I am proud of you. Why, you've even indented a paragraph. Now maybe you would like to put a margin on the page and then put it in the file tonight. I'll talk about it with you tomorrow."

She stood looking at me as if to say, "Well, aren't you going to scold me, or aren't you going to say anything?"

I just returned her look, my eyes never wavering, and she went back to her seat. I lost track of her during the rest of the day, but after school I could hardly wait to see what she had done with her paper.

When I took the paper out of the file that night it said, "Dear Mrs. Kapp, I love you. You are the only friend I have. I know you love me."

Chapter Three

"I Never Knowed the World Looked So Good"

I t was Friday afternoon, the end of April, and nearing the end of the school year. Aromas from the lunchroom wafted across the hall to room 16, carried on the slight breeze through the open window near my desk. I usually kept that window ajar, to provide a relief from the warm, sweaty young bodies that would come bounding into the room after recess. At this time of year the children seemed to be trying to shake off winter and free their spirits by running like untamed colts in the meadow behind the school.

There were other signs of spring. The girls' dresses showed evidence of hems let out to help cover spindly legs that seemed to be attached only at the waist. The faded and well-worn shirts and pants of the boys matched the sun-bleached pictures mounted on the bulletin board, with the many pin holes in the corners revealing much use throughout the year.

As I slowly and nostalgically rested my eyes on each student, I knew where to look for the broken and chewed-off pencils, the dog-eared notebooks, and also the neat and tidy desks. The smell of chalk dust from neglected boards and brushes, together with the hum of the motor from the boiler room next door, seemed to impose a heaviness of routine that must be broken to release these captured students.

What curriculum did I really have a responsibility for? To whom was I really accountable? Was arithmetic more important than witnessing new life in the spring?

I got up from my desk, erased the assignment on the chalkboard, and announced, "Please put your pencils down and follow me quickly. I would like you to bring with you the gifts God has given each one of you."

While many looked puzzled, some curious, and others surprised, only Becky spoke out in a questioning voice, "What are we supposed to bring?"

Pleased by her usual eagerness to be obedient, I explained that in the springtime there are sounds to hear, new growth to touch, smells to enjoy, beauties to see and even taste. We were going outside to experience spring with our eyes, nose, mouth, hands, and ears.

All of the students, even Kevin, seemed to feel the anticipation of this experiment. And so, like birds freed from a cage, they were released to the out-of-doors even though it wasn't recess or lunchtime.

By agreement we did little talking—just pointing, showing, uncovering, discovering, sharing, listening, and touching. Then we returned to the classroom bearing such treasures and gifts as are not seen by many. This time the room was quiet, but filled with new life and spring, and each child eagerly tried to capture on paper his experience. All of the students seemed to be flooding with ideas to be expressed, limited only by the mechanics of writing. All, that is, except Christine. I walked by her desk and glanced at her blank paper and her tightly clenched fist holding her pencil, then turned quickly away to relieve any pressure caused when a teacher stands too close.

My curiosity led me to Bradley's desk. What would this high-spirited, tousle-haired youth have to say? His experience outdoors seemed quite unlike him, for he just sat daydreaming and staring at the sky. To my surprise, he had already filled several lines on his paper, and I asked if he would share them with me. Pushing the paper toward me he said, "Sure, I'll read it to you." With a statement of declaration he read the title, "Blue." Then he continued, "I like blue because it makes you feel you are in a place that never ends. It is like a thing you touch and go right through. It is clear and nice. It seemed like you can fall right through blue."

With that last line his voice seemed to transport him again into the outdoors, into a world that only Bradley felt for sure. I whispered thanks to him for helping me to see the sky in a special way. Inside I gave thanks that I had not interrupted his daydreaming and prodded him to see what I saw.

Moving to the other side of the room, I responded to Kimberly's excitement as she raised one hand to its full height to get my attention and waved her paper in the other. She wanted to read her masterpiece to me. "Spring is a wonderful time of the year. I can feel, I can see, I can taste, and I can hear." Her rhyme continued on for two full pages, expressing her excitement for spring.

From the back of the room I looked again at Christine, her matted hair, her faded, too short dress with the belt held together with a large safety pin, her elbows chappy from lack of care. She was a little girl who said she liked fourth grade because when she came late her teacher didn't yell at her but just said in a quiet voice, "I'm glad you made it, Christine."

Wondering what she might write that could be reflective of hope and spring, I felt sorry for putting her in a situation to struggle for such expression. Just then she turned to see where I was, and I recognized that familiar look in her eyes that said, "Could you come here?" When I reached her desk, the tight grip on her pencil seemed to be squeezing out the last letter of her message. I glanced at her smudged paper, worn through in one spot from too much erasing. Her simple message was, "I never knowed the world looked so good."

Her freckled face was reaching upward with the faint smile of success for an experience that she knew was special. She eagerly awaited my response. With clouded eyes and on bended knee, I looked into her face and saw a new smile, bordered with chapped lips, and I whispered, "Thank you, thank you, Christine. I never knowed the world looked so good either."

Chapter Four

Strained Friendship

*I*had watched them at play
for several days and at first, only by very careful observation,
could I catch just a glimpse now and then of quiet hurting
that comes when friendship is strained.

Early in the year Luann and Karen had chosen to sit by
each other in school and by special request had served on
several committees together. It was mid-year now, and while
there had been some ups and downs, as might be expected
even with good friends, during the past month they had each
enjoyed the luxury of having a friend as a source of strength
to help in overcoming the bumps that constantly loom up
during the growing-up years.

I had learned through years of teaching young people
that days are sweet and all is well when you have the
assurance of a good friend, one who will choose you first if
she's captain, and who, if you have to remain after school,
will be waiting for you just outside the door, reminding you
that you're important. Some teachers try to separate friends
in class to cut down on the talking, but keeping friendships
alive and communication open seems more vital than a quiet
classroom, providing the lessons are learned and the objec-
tives for being in school are reached.

I first noticed the strained relationship between Luann
and Karen during a bulletin board project in which they
were planning a current-events display. Karen carefully put a
letter up, placed the pin neatly in the corner, and then
stepped back to admire her work. When Luann, trying to ap-
pear casual, reached up to adjust the carefully placed letter

just a little, Karen shrugged her shoulders, left the project, and returned to her seat with an "I don't care" attitude.

Watching from my desk, I noted once again that actions that are intended to show you don't care are often evidence of deep caring and hurting inside. One friend gained or lost during the school year may not seem that important during a child's fourth-grade experience, unless that experience could be used to pave the way for developing those important attributes that ensure lasting friendships in years to come. Childish behaviors developed as children are too often replayed by adults without a knowledge of a better way, and friendships that might otherwise be treasured possessions are strained, if not lost.

During the previous few weeks, I had observed the girls on the playground, in the lunchroom, during reading groups, and especially when they were alone together, which they seemed now to be avoiding. They no longer wore the dresses that they had purposely had their mothers make alike. Instead of just a childhood friendship that was quick in forming and just as quick in passing, this was not passing—it was growing in hurt. When two people hurt together, a certain sharing takes place that is binding in spite of intended rejection. What is interpreted by youth as hate is really a hurting because of love for so much shared by each other. Love grows from risking, taking down the protective covering, and opening our inner thoughts and feelings, sharing our very self, whether as a child or an adult. While the circumstances are different, the hurt is much the same.

How might Luann and Karen find a way, not just to preserve this friendship but, more important, to learn the way, the path to lasting friendships? This seemed like the teaching moment for such a lesson, and it was important that it not be bypassed, even at the expense of other lessons, including arithmetic, reading, and social studies.

A vivid memory of my own childhood provided a gift of understanding for the hurting that troubled friendship can cause. When I was ten years old, my best friend, who was president of our very select club, announced that I was to be "let out of the club." Apparently my suggestion that we take turns being president had not been well received, and the club members rallied around the president. I remember the awful feeling, the lonesome ache inside that seemed to come so suddenly and be so overpowering as the girls gathered around the president and I was left standing alone. I had to do something.

My mother's little country store was halfway down the gravel road between the school and the last stop as each one left the group to go home. I recall walking fast ahead of my friends, and then an idea came into my mind. I began running. I jumped the irrigation ditch, ran through the meadow past the old church, past the picket fence in front of Bucks, where the gooseberry bushes pushed through the slats, by the pasture where the cows were grazing in the late afternoon sun, and finally around the corner. I stopped to catch my breath just before entering the door into the back supply room of the store. There, just as I remembered, were boxes of candy bars. I couldn't take time to explain to Mom why I needed eight bars and besides, she might say no, and I had to have them. I could hear her busy with customers in the store so I decided to carry out my plan without approval. Besides, I rationalized, it was our store, so it wasn't really wrong to take the bars.

By carefully climbing on a case of canned corn I was able to reach the bars. I took eight; I didn't need one for myself—just one for each of my would-be friends. Luckily my jacket had pockets, and with four bars tucked in each pocket, I ran back just as the girls were approaching the corner by the old garage.

Hoping beyond hope, I offered each of the girls a bar. Right after school is a good time to be tempted with a treat, and immediately my plan was successful. One of the girls suggested that they take another vote, and just that quickly I was a member of the club again.

I remember not feeling very good about taking the candy, and the next day at school when the candy bars had been eaten and forgotten, I began to feel unsure again about my place in the club. Something awakened in me the realization that there has to be a better way to make and keep friends, so that when the sweetness of the candy is forgotten, the sweetness of friendship remains. Eventually I talked to Mom about the candy bars and she seemed to understand, but she explained that while I was right in trying to work out the problem myself, the solution must come from good feelings inside that others couldn't resist, rather than from bribes in candy bars. She further explained, "If you can always have warm feelings inside, others will eventually respond the same way."

One morning, very early, when I went with Dad to build the fire in the coal stove in the store, I really learned the meaning of her lesson. Dad seemed to sense my left-out feeling with the group, and I suspect his heart was hurting for the suffering he could not protect me from. I sat on a nail keg near the stove with my coat wrapped around me. As he began cutting kindling for the fire, he talked to me about my friends and my responsibilities to like them in spite of my membership in the club. Then he changed the subject, or so I thought. "Ardie," he said, "we'd like this old stove to give us some heat, wouldn't we." As I shivered in the cold Canadian morning, I agreed.

"It would be easier to do this job if it was warm, wouldn't it," he said. (He was kindling the fire and I could see his breath even though his head was ducked.) I agreed.

Then came the lesson. "You see, Ardie, we have to put in the wood before we get the heat. If we wait for the warmth of the fire before we do our part, we'll have to wait a long time." After a lesson like that, Dad always quit talking and waited for the learning to take place. As I watched him crumple the paper and place the kindling in the stove and the larger pieces of wood carefully on top, leaving air space, I thought of my friends and how I was waiting for them to like me. Finally, when he lit the match and the kindling took fire, almost immediately we stood side by side, rubbing our hands and feeling the warmth.

I don't remember much else about that experience, but it must have worked out, because I do recall having had a turn at being president of the club. Could I somehow, many years later, help Luann and Karen learn the importance of putting in the wood that would give the warmth they each so much needed at this time, to heal the hurting inside?

It was late afternoon. Our classroom was on the west side

of the building, and the warm rays of the sun were beating down on asphalt just outside the window near my desk. Something about the warmth of the sun seemed to be the key. Following recess, I decided to try a plan. Calling Karen and Luann to my side as the other students hurried back into the class, I took them over by the curb that separated the lawn from the asphalt and asked them to sit down, one on each side of me. They sat with their heads turned away from each other. Sitting between them, I tried to reason with them, but nothing seemed to work. Finally, something from the long ago flashed into my mind. My mother had said the solution has to come from inside, and you have to work it out yourself. I stood up, looked at each of them, and quietly said, "Rather than doing your regular assignments today, I would like you to do your lessons out here. Would you talk things over, and when you have everything worked out and you feel good inside about each other, come and get me and make a report."

Though her head was turned, I saw Karen's jaw tighten, giving evidence of clenched teeth. Luann flipped her long blonde curls as she adjusted her position, placing her back squarely in the opposite direction. I left them alone and returned to class. Frequently I walked over to the window. Fifteen minutes later their positions had changed only slightly; Karen now sat with her knees under her chin and her arms wrapped firmly around her legs, in an "I won't move" sort of position, and Luann had now shifted around a little, drawing lines with her finger in the loose dirt on the edge of the curb. Just as I was about to turn away, Luann, with her head still turned in the opposite direction, moved her feet in the direction of shortening that ominous distance that separated her from Karen. Then she quickly shifted her body along the curb and mastered about ten inches, but still she didn't look toward her friend. I noticed a large rock about halfway between the two girls, and that became the point of determining who was making the greatest progress in the restoration of this friendship.

Sometime later I saw that the rock was still between the girls, but the distance between them was much shorter. While the challenge of looking at each other was still too much, they were both talking as they looked at their feet.

During the next hour the demands of the classroom took my full attention, and it wasn't until near the end of the day that I witnessed their great victory. Still sitting on the curb but now side by side, each of them had one arm around the other's neck, and both were talking at once. They had solved their problem themselves from the inside, and the warmth of the sun in the out-of-doors must have helped.

Soon there was a knock on my door. I looked quickly out the window and saw that the girls were gone. Going to the door I opened it, and there were these two friends, holding hands and both saying at once, "It's okay now." I could see that it was, but I wanted more. Closing the door behind me, I stood in the hall, ready to receive a full account. "Tell me about it," I said.

They looked at each other and smiled, and Luann spoke first. "Well, in family home evening this week, my dad said you're supposed to like your enemies." Still holding hands, Karen interrupted to explain, "In our family home evening, my dad said you're supposed to *love* your enemies." Again, wanting more details of this little miracle, I said, "Tell me what happened." Karen, with her arm once again around Luann's neck, said, "Well, we do," and Luann quickly confirmed the message: "Yes, we do."

While I stood savoring the sweetness of that moment, they were ready to return to class and get on with their activities together.

Love is the strongest force in the world, and when it is blocked, pain results. We can kill the love so that it stops hurting, but then, of course, part of us dies too. Or we can ask God to open up another route for that love to travel. We can remember the Savior's words: "Love your enemies." (Matthew 5:44.)

Chapter 5

"I Wish I'd Said That"

$\mathcal{M}$iss Nielson was just quieting the students after recess as I walked into the second grade classroom at the Washington Elementary School. The regular teacher had left the room for several hours to allow Miss Nielson, the student teacher, the opportunity to feel like a real teacher and manage the class by herself.

I quietly took my customary seat in the back of the room on one of only two full-sized chairs in the entire classroom. There I found the lesson plan marked Language Arts neatly prepared and placed in a folder lying on the countertop near the sink awaiting the student teaching supervisor.

This would be a good day for Miss Nielson. There was evidence of thorough preparation in every detail. I sensed a feeling of excitement and anticipation on the part of this very sensitive, capable young woman. She obviously had the interest of each child in mind and seemed anxious to share a learning experience with them.

Miss Nielson, looking more like a student herself than a teacher, skillfully used a variety of teaching techniques to gain the full attention of each second grader. With all eyes on her she responded with a twinkle in her eye and a soft, expressive voice.

"Today I'm going to tell you some stories." I glanced quickly at the lesson plan in the folder to determine the objective of such an approach even though it was always a sure way to hold the interest of second graders. According to instruction, at the top of the lesson plan in bold letters was the heading "Lesson Objective," and a brief statement followed: "Upon completion of this lesson each student will demonstrate his or her ability for comprehension by expressing appropriate responses to selected stories."

Soon I found myself joining the children and being carried away by the magic of a good storyteller, and in response there was the music of their laughter and their refreshing interpretation as they expressed their feelings and revealed some indication of understanding.

Miss Nielson demonstrated her most valuable attribute as a teacher as she genuinely showed respect for each child's point of view. She listened intently as Becky, one of the better readers, discussed with Brad, one of the strong-willed ones, whether the statement in the story "he went to bed with the chickens" meant that he went to bed early or, as Brad insisted, "he really slept with the chickens."

Twenty minutes slipped away quickly, as it always does with a good teacher, and the students were still eagerly listening, responding, and asking for "just one more." As though this was all part of her plan, with the end in mind, she led them toward the final teaching moment and carefully prepared them for the last story. "Boys and girls," she began, eyes sweeping the entire group and including each child, "I'm going to tell you a story about two different neighbors, and after the stories I'd like you to think about their characteristics and tell how you feel."

Several of the students showed concern for that big word, *characteristics,* until Miss Nielson gave a simple explanation that left them feeling eager about the challenge.

There was a Mr. Brown, she began, the friendliest man in town. She told in great detail how he knew everybody's name, including the children, and how he would take time to fix a broken wheel on a worn-out wagon or tricycle. He could make whistles out of dandelion stems and flippers from the branches of trees, and could tell you the names of all the birds.

Then, with the full description of Mr. Brown well-implanted in the hearts and minds of the children, the teacher paused a moment to change the mood before introducing poor old Mr. Black. Dropping her voice and frowning slightly, she explained that everyone knew him, especially the children. They knew him best of all. Then the full description of Mr. Black came to life as they could see in their minds the details of the story.

As children would walk past his house, they could see him through the broken picket fence sitting alone in an old chair on his porch. The only time they saw him move was when one of the older kids would dare someone to shout at him, open his gate, or throw a rock onto his lawn; then he had a very loud voice and he would stand up and shake his fist. It was very clear that Mr. Black was a cross old man.

Closing the book, Miss Nielson smiled as she invited the responses to Mr. Brown. The enthusiastic comments from the students gave evidence of their identity with a newfound friend. Much discussion followed as each one added to and agreed with what had been said about Mr. Brown.

With the lesson nearing completion, and almost as an afterthought, Miss Nielson posed the question, "Who would like to be neighbor to Mr. Black?" There was silence for a few minutes, and there would be no response, so it seemed, until one little blond boy, who had been rather quiet, raised his hand hesitantly. The students sitting near him responded with a few childish snickers. The boy withdrew his hand ever so slightly, hesitated an instant as others joined in the snickering, and then, holding his hand steady, stretched it to full height and waited.

I glanced at Miss Nielson. This was not in the lesson plan. It was unrehearsed, unplanned for. The snickering continued, but the little lad looked straight ahead, his arm held high and his eyes on the teacher. Miss Nielson walked toward the boy's desk as if to lend him support.

Something in that moment changed the mood. The snickering stopped and the teacher simply said, "Jeff."

Jeff lowered his hand and nervously, with all eyes on him, said hesitantly, "I wish Mr. Black was my neighbor." Something about the way he said the words left everyone wanting to know and understand more. He went on, "I wish Mr. Black was my neighbor, because if he was my neighbor, my mom would make a pie for me to take to him." Then, with the confidence of maybe having experienced something like this before, he took his eyes from the teacher, looked at the children, and added with conviction, "and then he wouldn't be that way anymore."

A hush fell over the room. I watched Miss Nielson as she watched the children. Without interrupting the mood, she quietly closed her lesson plan with one hand, gently rested her other hand on Jeff's shoulder, and said almost reverently, "Thank you, Jeff, for that beautiful lesson."

I sensed the challenge of twenty-two second graders trying to give meaning to what they had just experienced.

I saw a young teacher lay aside her carefully prepared plan to make room for a better lesson.

I saw a child who was true to his convictions stand alone among his friends and teach a better way.

I took my pencil and wrote in bold letters on my copy of the lesson plan, next to "Objective," "Objective accomplished—appropriate response to selected story."

And then, almost as a benediction, the silence was broken by one child who spoke in a whisper just barely loud enough for all to hear, "I wish I'd said that."

Chapter 6

When We Are in the Service of Our Fellowman

*S*ome years ago near the close of day something happened in the lives of a group of wonderful young Mia Maid girls. Prior to that afternoon, hours had been spent in cookie making, trying new recipes, program planning, writing new songs, friendship building, and lots and lots of chatting — as I recall, much more chatting than listening. Any observer would agree that was an active activity, but one might also ask what of the principle being taught.

On the designated day all the plans for delivery of the cookies and presentations of the program were carried out as scheduled amid bubbling laughter, gaiety, and the enthusiasm of youth, everyone wanting to be a part of the action. The only flaw in the plan was that several good-sized bags of cookies were left when all the appointments had been filled. Now the question was what to do with the extra cookies. Several suggestions came at once, "We could eat them or take them to the Explorers or sell them."

Then the voice of the class president was heard, overriding the rest in a more thoughtful tone. "Let's see if there's an old folks home where grandpas live."

A call was made, an immediate appointment arranged, and a group of young girls stood at the front door of a large rest home, a little less enthusiastic now about what had seemed like a great idea. As the door was opened, each girl tried awkwardly to push behind the one in front so as not to be first. There was a moment of strain, with many thinking, "Why did we come?"

Three of the girls quickly unloaded the sacks of cookies on the old table that appeared to be the only piece of furniture in the room other than the beds and wheelchairs occupied by the patients. As the girls began singing one of the songs they had prepared, one or two shoulders were raised from slumped positions that had appeared to be permanent. A few patients in wheelchairs were pushed closer by other patients.

The girls continued singing, gaining a little more courage from the warm response. At that moment a miracle was taking place. The countenances were gradually but surely changing on the faces of the aged. Expressions were changing and eyes filling with tears as the youths began a different song. This time a foreign exchange student sang a song in German as the other girls hummed the familiar tune. Only then did a bent old man, slumped on the side of a bed visible through the doorway of an adjoining room, raise his head and in soft but audible tone join in the words of his native tongue. Heads were turned, eyes filled with tears, hearts were touched, and lives were changed. A few words of appreciation were expressed, and a different group of young girls walked quietly down the steps of the old building.

Oh, the thoughts that were shared by each during the trip home! One asked, in an inquiring tone, "What happened? I've never felt like this before." Another said, almost in a whisper, "When can we do it again?"

The girls and their leader experienced that day the message spoken of by John: "If any man will do his will, he shall know of the doctrine, whether it be of God, or whether I speak of myself." (John 7:17.) For that moment we were living a principle in a Christlike way, and we all thirsted for more. When we are in the service of our fellowmen, we are in the service of our God. That night we were in his service, and we felt his nearness.

Chapter 7

Fashion Show

*L*aurels Fashion Gay Paree" was the heading of the featured article on the center spread of the *Church News*. The article began, "The pretty and energetic Laurels of Bountiful 18th Ward started something that turned out big in the annals of fashion shows in Bountiful Stake—it was entitled 'Triumph in Fashion.'" While the newspaper article gave a glowing report of the event, the real triumph was never really reported except within the hearts of each one who participated.

It all began when twelve girls, ready to leave the Laurel class after having met together every week, and sometimes more often, for three years with the same teacher, decided they wanted to leave a gift in memory of their class. Through the years as Mia Maids and now Laurels they had developed an identity, a reputation, a unity and strength within the group, and they wanted to do something big with that power of unity, which they had learned to use in small ways and had depended on to strengthen one another. The extent of a person's power is unknown until it is tested, and the triumph comes when discovery of that power surpasses the limits of his expectations and he begins to catch a vision of the resources that are his for the asking.

Twelve girls sixteen and seventeen years of age, with their teacher, sat together on the lawn at the meetinghouse drinking root beer and eating doughnuts, wondering what they might do. Their teacher mused over the varieties of personalities within the group. Just three years ago when they had first met together as a class, one of them had commented,

"You don't have to bother to call and ask for my attendance. Just mark me absent at sacrament meeting, 'cause I never go and I never intend to." Each one came to the group like a piece of a jigsaw puzzle, unique and different, unlike in shape, in size, and in color. But each one was a vital part of the whole if it were put together carefully in the proper relationships without too much forcing that might mar the carefully designed edges. This girl did eventually come, and so did each of the others.

In a close-knit group that has learned to work together, a simple idea dropped by one is picked up by another, added to and expanded by still another, until finally everyone has added a bit and no one really knows for sure where the idea got its start. With the strength of a group dreams can be much higher than when one dreams alone. Together a group can overcome tremendous obstacles. With the resources available to each girl in the group, the combined possibilities seemed exciting; but these resources had never yet been really explored, much less brought into action.

As the girls talked, they decided to organize and present a very special fashion show for all the youth of the ward. The teacher, observing their eagerness to do together more than they could possibly do alone, was reminded of the coyote that streaks across the prairie at 35 miles an hour and also of the rabbit that can run at close to 45 miles an hour; yet how many times she had known of coyotes, through uniting their resources and working together, overcoming the challenge of that arithemetic and overtaking the rabbit. The first coyote takes after the rabbit and chases him in the direction of the second coyote, and then the second one takes up the chase at an angle that allows the first to take a shortcut at a leisurely pace while he gets his wind back before he takes up the chase again.

While the example had little to do with the exciting chatter about a fashion show, still the analogy seemed to have increasingly apparent meaning. Plans were made, committees were assigned, and a report-back meeting was scheduled in three days. After that, each meeting became an enlargement and expansion of the original plan. It was when the girls decided on a luncheon for all the girls and women in the ward, in addition to the fashion show, that they had to expand their resources. One of the girls began to break the barrier that seemed to limit their dreams when she proposed an idea: "Why don't each of us have our moms serve on the committee we're responsible for?" Some thought it was a great idea and readily volunteered their mothers' help. Others were more hesitant. "I don't know if I want to work on a committee with my mother. We don't really get along all that well." But when the strength of these expanded resources was considered, it was unanimous that every girl would at least ask her mother and report back next week.

The responses reported at the next meeting really changed the challenge. Each mother had agreed to help— including one mother who had never even been inside the church but who now agreed to be a member of the committee of which her daughter would be chairman.

This added support gave wings to even bigger and better ideas. "Why don't we invite the whole stake?" asked the girl who was in charge of the ticket sales. "I think we ought to build a big ramp to extend from the stage clear out into the cultural hall," was the recommendation of the fashion show chairman. The decorating committee member caught the vision and suggested red carpeting to cover the ramp and large plants to line both sides of it.

Once again the girls' plans had expanded beyond their resources, but cutting back was never a consideration. They took stock of available backup resources, the extent of which they were just beginning to realize. One girl confidently assured the others, "I know my dad will help us. He has a truck, and he knows lots of people." When the teacher, having caught the vision of these undaunted youth, volunteered that her husband would build the ramp, she was thinking only of the labor and not the lumber—an inconsequential detail. Almost immediately every father was volunteered, as each girl assured the others that her dad would help. This was a bit doubtful, since some of the fathers had not given any indication of wanting to be involved in *any* church activity, but to these girls, nothing seemed impossible.

Their resources continued to stretch to carry the load that enlarged with every meeting. There seemed to be no bounds to their ideas. Mothers were volunteering sons, and fathers were recommending priesthood quorum members. "Why, you could have male waiters wearing white shirts and black bow ties," was a suggestion from one father. "Why don't you ask the high priests to serve?" another suggested. By now the luncheon committee could hardly keep pace with the ticket sales. The size of the ramp had to be shortened to allow room for more and more tables.

With such interest in the event, the program committee reevaluated their efforts and decided such an elaborate affair would surely justify a celebrity to announce the fashions and be the show's moderator. The girls learned that Rosemarie Reed, an internationally known fashion designer, was visiting in Orem, Utah. With the power and strength of the group supporting them, they felt free to take wings with confidence. They contacted Rosemarie Reed, and she accepted.

Throughout the weeks preceding the event, the only detail that remained constant was the date, and when it finally arrived, the events unfolded as planned and with all the girls' dreams fulfilled. Mothers and fathers, brothers and sisters were there to support their own Laurels. The stake presidency, members of the high council, and many fathers took their places as waiters just as the girls had envisioned, each dressed in black pants, bow tie, and white shirt, and with a towel over the left arm.

Red carpet covered the entire stage and the full length of the ramp, which also had live trees down both sides. The 530 guests were seated at tables that featured a French decor, with beautiful flowers arranged in the center of each. Following a delicious luncheon, the models gracefully stepped through the *Arc de Triomphe* portrayed on the curtain as Rosemarie Reed described the fashions. She also bore testimony of the importance of the Church in her life and related faith-promoting incidents as she introduced the models in the fashion parade.

The following Sunday morning, as requested by the stake presidency, the twelve Laurels and their teacher met at eight o'clock with the stake presidency and high council at the stake center. It was a very special experience for each girl, especially when the class president presented $700 to the stake president with a brief explanation. "This is to be used as you see fit for the Bountiful Stake recreation center," she said. "It is a gift to those who follow us from this year's Eighteenth Ward Laurel class."

With obvious emotion, the stake president leaned back in his chair and said, "Tell us how you did it."

It was not until then that the full realization of what had happened fell into place. As each girl reported on the activities of her own committee, the event was finally summarized, for each one said, in essence, "When we had our family behind us, supporting us and working with us, we had fun in working together. And it seemed as though there wasn't anything we couldn't do."

Chapter 8

Bridges of Friendship

*I*n Hobart, Tasmania, on a beautiful wintery night, a group of young women had come from miles around to meet together in the home of one of their leaders. It was the first time many of them had met each other, so it was quite natural they would be sitting and talking with those whom they already knew and enjoying the security of friendships already established. There seemed to be an obvious distance between the groups, even though the room was relatively small and they were seated not far from each other.

As a backdrop to this setting, a large picture window with the drapes open wide revealed the beautiful city around us. Twinkling lights from the houses on the hills to the east seemed to be responding to the lights on the west, like studded jewels. Between the two hills was a large dark area. That area, I was told, was the Derwent River, but there was no evidence of a bridge, no lights, no signs of anything spanning the gap.

Then I remembered having heard about the disaster that took place at 9:27 P.M. on Sunday, January 5, 1975, when the Australian liner *Lake Illawarra* collided with the Tasman Bridge and sank. The ship, having lost its way, went off course and collided with piers 18 and 19, and the deck span they supported collapsed into the river, breaking the major connection between the portions of the city separated by the river. And so, without the lights on the bridge to signify the connecting link, the distance separating the city lights seemed very large.

My attention was then drawn back to the girls in the room, still talking within their own groups. Between these young girls there was not yet a bridge to span the gap that separated them, nothing to tie them together.

The leader had asked a representative of each group to report how many girls were enrolled in her class and how many attended regularly. As each responded, there seemed to be a vast difference between the number enrolled and those who attended. And when attention was drawn to the fact that it was not just numbers but actual, real people they were talking about, there was evidence of increased concern. Now they were talking about girls for whom they had a great responsibility..

As this thought was seriously considered and better understood, the girls, with the help of a wise leader, began talking among themselves first and then with the girls in the other groups. They began looking beyond themselves for answers in their desire to reach out to others. Could anyone help—did anyone in the room have any ideas? Could they together, with the ideas of many, come up with a plan to reach those girls who now seemed out of reach?

Listening to their youthful chatter and enthusiasm with everyone now talking to each other and sometimes several talking at once, I thought again of the Tasman Bridge and the restoration and reconstruction plans I had read about. Was there a similarity here? A proposal had been made to bridge the river gap by repairing and strengthening some piers while constructing others. This would necessitate constructing temporary steel towers around the columns to support the existing spans while restoration took place. The plan was approved, a decision was made, and a target date for completion of the Tasman Bridge was set for the end of 1977.

Again I turned my attention to the girls and watched carefully their interaction and felt their concern. That night I witnessed bridge builders—not bridges to span a river, not bridges to reach land, but bridges to span the area between human souls reaching out to one another in search of ways to stretch and reach even into the unknown.

"I don't even know if all the girls are on our rolls," said

one. "We can check it out with our ward clerk," said another. "We're in different schools and she never comes to church, so how can I see her?" was another comment.

With much conversation and concern now, the time passed quickly. After some refreshments were served, a closing prayer was offered. Included in the prayer was a plea for success in "reaching the other girls." Chattering enthusiastically, the girls, now unidentifiable by groups, made their way down the stairs and out into the street.

The following evening at one of the wards, just before the meeting was to begin, two girls whom I recognized from the night before rushed up to give an accounting. Both were talking at once as they reported how they had checked all of the names of the girls in their class, had already written a letter to each of them, and had made plans to include the other members of the class in visiting those whom they wished to reach. Their countenances revealed intense concern for those for whom they felt responsibility. These were the steel towers that would support the columns for the bridge to span the gap that would tie one human soul to another. But not just one bridge or even two were built that night; many, many bridges were in the making.

Several weeks later an air mail letter arrived at my home with a Tasmanian postmark. The letter read, in part: "I am not sure whether you remember me, but I was one of the Laurel presidents. After that night I got really inspired and filled with the spirit, and I can't really remember when I had felt like that before. That night I went home and prayed to my Father in heaven and asked for strength to help our inactive Laurels want to come back. That night I felt a real peace over my soul—and I realized how powerful and wonderful the Holy Ghost is. I immediately wrote to my girls and I got only one reply; she was sick and couldn't make it to class, but I'll be seeing her soon. Another girl didn't come at first but I told her she could stay at my home, and now we meet each other after work. She has been sustained as secretary now. . . . I realize the importance of my responsibility, how one day I will have to answer to the Lord. I am going to press on and work with my leaders. I am not going to live on a borrowed testimony; I am going to get my own through hard work."

Since that night in Tasmania, I have watched carefully the silent, quiet, unnoticed work of many bridge builders.

Going through my mail one day I noticed two air mail letters, both with stamps from a far-away place I had recently visited. I opened the first letter and it began: "I hope you can remember me, I'm _____." A page of details followed to make sure I knew the writer, a young girl. She poured her heart out about her concern for her "separated family," as she explained it. She told of her desire to be strong and her urgent need for a trusted friend. And then she closed with this comment: "Well, I'll let you go now, and I'm sorry if I took up too much of your time." I thought of this young girl so far away, and so much in need of a close friend. What kind of a bridge could reach from here to there and span the gap?

Then I opened the other letter. This one began, "May I ask for some cookies? (She meant help and advice.) I'm not really sure where to start, but here goes. I am very concerned for my friend," and she gave the friend's name. Immediately I picked up the first letter and checked the signature and the unusual spelling of the name. It was the same girl who had written to ask for help! I read on and felt the deep concern expressed by one young girl for the welfare of another: "I have prayed about it, but how can I tell her of my concern for her exaltation? Maybe I am not being a good enough friend to her. Do you have any suggestions?"

Two letters, and each girl unaware of the correspondence of the other—one reaching out to help and the other asking for help, and each one answering the other's need. Both letters were answered, giving gentle direction that would hopefully turn them to each other with the trust and concern that would form a bridge, one that would eventually become a strong tie over which they could each safely pass.

Whenever a bridge is gently and carefully built, someone will sometime cautiously and trustingly cross over it, although in some cases it may be even years later.

A few months ago I spent a short time as a patient in the hospital. One night about midnight I was awakened when I heard someone whisper, "Sister Kapp." It was not until I heard the words the second time that I opened my eyes and saw a young girl standing by the side of my bed. Her uniform

30

told me that she was a nurse's aide, but why this midnight visit, and why the formal salutation? Still half asleep, I wondered about the seeming uncertainty of her voice as she leaned down and quietly whispered, "Could I sit on the edge of your bed and talk to you for a few minutes?" Somewhat surprised, I said yes. Then she told me how five years before, when I was speaking to a large group of young women, I had expressed a desire to speak to them as individuals. I had told them how I used to sit on the edge of my sister's bed and we would chat for hours, and how I wished I might sit on the edge of their beds so we could open our hearts to each other and really communicate.

By now I had moved over, leaving enough room on the bed for her to sit very close. As I reached for her hand, she continued: "I thought then how very much I would like to have you sit on the edge of my bed. I had so many things I wanted to talk to someone about." Even in the dimly lit room I could see her serious countenance. She went on, "When I came on night shift and saw your name in the files, I hurried to see if it could possibly be you, hoping I might have the chance I so much wanted five years ago. So here I am—I hope it's okay."

That night a bridge that began years before was trustingly crossed, and there in the semidarkened room, a young girl opened her heart and told of her weighty decisions, her need for encouragement, and her desire to do right. After several hours, which seemed very brief, the morning sun began filtering through the blind on the window. Who was in fact the patient and who was the nurse's aide that night? Another bridge spanned the distance between two human souls and both were lifted.

"This is what the world is waiting for: bridges—bridges of friendship." (Thomas John Carlyle)

Chapter Nine

"I Will See You Up There"

I had been invited to speak at a standards night for handicapped young women in Bountiful, Utah. In preparation for the assignment I felt an urgency to help these young women have a feeling of self-esteem and self-worth. It seemed very important that each one be called by name. I did not know how many young women there might be, but before leaving home I prayed earnestly that I might be able, contrary to my normal ability, to call each one by name. I also took a large bag full of visual aids and props to help in sustaining their very short attention span.

At the meetinghouse I was met by Sister Harriet Sheffield, one of the faithful leaders who work with these precious souls. We went into the chapel, where a song practice for both the young men and young women was being held. Sister Sheffield and I took our seats in front of the audience. Responding to my request, she identified the young women sitting among the adult leaders and parents, going up and down each row, telling me the name of each of the girls.

When song practice was concluded, the mothers, daughters, and leaders were asked to go to the Relief Society room, where a lace cloth covered the table, with beautifully arranged flowers, a buffet table at the side, and other details to make the setting feminine and special.

There was a lovely spirit among these young women. I again prayed fervently that I might be able to teach by the spirit and remember their names. The evening began with the youth singing "I Am a Child of God," and somehow in that setting the words seemed to have greater meaning than ever.

When I stood to speak, I explained to them that our Father in heaven knows each girl by name. I began by telling them that he knows Jill, he knows Joyce, and he knows Marin. As I mentioned their names, each girl would look surprised and turn around, look at the others, sit up taller, and whisper, "How does she know my name?" Then I told them that if I could know their names, could they imagine how much more our Father in heaven would know about them, how he would know how they felt inside, when they were happy and when they were unhappy, and how much he cared.

I asked if there were any of them who had ever felt as if they were hurting inside. Most of them raised their hands, and we discussed how everyone in that room—in fact, every one of our Father's children—has times when they feel as if they are hurting inside. This is a time when we can grow very close to our Father in heaven because he knows how we feel, and he loves us and will always be there to help us and strengthen us.

The first visual aid I used was the one of Elder Boyd K. Packer's in which he used the hand to represent the eternal spirit and a glove to represent the body that houses the spirit. (*Teach Ye Diligently,* Deseret Book, 1975, p. 232.)

We looked around and observed how lovely the girls looked in their beautiful dresses, and they really did. Then we discovered that the important thing that made them look so radiant was their beautiful, healthy, wonderful spirits inside. I bore testimony of the beauty of their spirits and their valor and faithfulness when they lived with their Father in heaven, as evidenced by their very existence. Each one seemed responsive to the fact that it is the spirit inside that we must help to grow and become beautiful. If we cut our finger and leave a scar on the outside, that isn't important so long as we don't wound our spirit and cause scars that do not heal on the inside.

We discussed the importance of developing good habits and knowing that what we are doing now determines what we will become. Then, calling them each by name, I asked Vicki, Jill, and Judy to come forward and take some packages from a large bag. In the bag were packages of flower, cabbage, and onion seeds. Following my instructions, each girl role-played planting the seeds. I asked what would happen, after the seeds were grown, if Vicki, who planted the onion seeds, wanted to be able, like Judy, to pick some flowers. They all responded, "Pick onion." She must pick what she planted. Together we discovered a true principle.

The importance of proper dress and the need to look modest and feminine were emphasized by suggesting that one can tell by looking at a person where that person is going. To demonstrate this thought, several of the girls were asked to respond as certain items were taken out of the bag. The first was a nightgown, and together they responded, "Going to bed." The next was a swimming suit, and they said, in unison, "Going swimming." Finally, I took out a book, and again they called out together, "You are going to read a book." We discovered that by looking at people and at what they are wearing or taking with them, we can usually tell where they are planning to go. And so it is with those who are planning to return to our Father in heaven. Their appearance is an indication of their intentions.

Sandra was sitting on the front row, and I called her by name and asked her to stand. I complimented her on her shiny hair and her lovely, modest dress. Sandra became an example for each of us not only in her dress, but in the expression on her face, which revealed her inner beauty. It was obvious by her appearance that she was striving to one day return to her Father in heaven. I thanked her for her example, and she sat down.

By now each of the girls seemed to be waiting to see if I would call her by name. As her name was called, each one responded the same. She would sit up tall and whisper, "She knows my name."

We talked about how our Father in heaven expects us to help and strengthen each other, and how we must be responsible for each other. This was demonstrated by suggesting that if Vicki was feeling bad or having a problem and felt that she was going the wrong way, she could depend on a friend to take her by the hand and steer her in the right direction. I then took Vicki's hand and guided her from her seat to the front of the table. She was smiling and holding back slightly as I pulled her forward. I stopped and put my arm around her, explaining that sometime I might need someone to help me go where I should go. "What can I do?" I asked. "Who can help me?" All of the girls responded, "Vicki pull her." Vicki held my hand tightly and began to pull me to the other side. In that moment as I felt the strength of her little hand pulling me forward and realized the sweetness and purity of her spirit, I experienced new insight into the words, ". . . and a little child shall lead them." (Isaiah 11:6.)

Then I told them how much we all need each other and how much they helped to pull me into the right path by their example and the radiance of their spirits, which could be felt by everyone present.

I had been asked to include some comments on how to show love and appreciation for someone without clinging and hanging onto them. I suggested that when we grow up to be young ladies, we don't hang onto each other quite so much. We can be very close and feel the warm spirit of friendship even without touching. I asked Linda, in a pretty red jumper, to stand close beside me. She tipped her head up and our eyes met. "Linda," I said, "can you feel that I love you?" There was a pause and I waited. At that moment I felt a great love for this child I hardly knew. She nodded her head and whispered and said, "I love you." For just a fleeting second, almost like a divine echo, I sensed that I was standing by the side of a very important person. Although that precious feeling was only momentary, it was very real, and I did love Linda and yearned to know the real Linda—the spirit that is housed only temporarily in a defective body.

As I looked into the faces of these precious young women and saw them sitting in their long dresses, they were truly beautiful. I noticed that Arlysa, Shari, and Judy were sitting tall on the front row, but each girl's youth was apparent in her feet exposed below her long dress, one toe of her shoe crossed over the other, pigeon-toe style. During that hour we laughed together, we cried together, and we all felt the spirit of our Father in heaven. In closing I bore testimony that we can live for any blessing that we want because our Father in heaven has promised that those who love him and keep his commandments shall receive all that he has.

I felt impressed to ask the girls if anyone would like to share with us a blessing she would like to live for. At this moment little Marin, a paraplegic with two artificial legs, who had just received a camp award that included participation in a lengthy hike, raised her hand. With a radiant, happy smile, she said, "I want to be able to skip the rope." There was silence for a moment, and I searched the eyes of all the adults present. At that moment we were taught a great lesson, and tears filled the eyes of many.

Then Judy, who seemed to be not so agile as some of the others, responded, "I want to jump." And Arlysa, sitting on the front row, said, in muffled and somewhat garbled words, "Set the table."

I told them on that occasion that I knew in my heart that one day they would skip the rope, jump, and set the table. I prayed that I too might be numbered with them to be worthy of receiving the righteous desires of my heart.

Finally, I asked Debbie and Joyce to come from the back row. I suggested that since they knew their friends, they might be able to suggest things that would help their friends to grow spiritually strong and beautiful. I waited for Joyce as she stood there for several moments. I wondered if I had called on one who was not able to respond because of some verbal limitation. Then finally she raised her head and said, "Love."

While limited by verbal expression, this child taught us by the spirit the greatest message of all—love for one another. At that moment there was a feeling of pure love of which each one partook and shared.

Then, with the hour spent and every girl having participated, I bore a final testimony, and prayer was offered. Afterwards Judy came forward with a smile and said, "You are my friend, and I will see you up there," pointing with her little thumb heavenward. In my heart I responded to her challenge as I made a pledge to strive harder to be there with her and the others one day.

Chapter Ten

"I Knew He Knew
I Was There"

Camp Piuta, high in Utah's Uinta Mountains, is one of my favorite places. It is fun to be there in the winter when the tall pine trees are packed with snow and the drifts around the lodge are so high that you have to climb to the top and slide down the snow into the narrow space between the lodge and the drift to get inside the lodge. It is fun in the rain when the smell of the pines is mingled with the smell of burning logs. But best of all, it is fun to hear the voices of happy girls ring through the trees and see squirrels scurry away as their playground is invaded by visitors.

It was early in the morning and the sun was just peeking over the tallest mountain. Nestled among the towering pine trees was a group of young girls, a little sleepy after having pushed and pulled their handcarts several miles up a steep, rocky incline the day before so that "we can get the real feeling of our pioneers." As we finally pulled the last handcart to the appointed place for camp, the expressions from many of the girls indicated that the objective of the camp was already accomplished.

The sun inched across the blue sky until dusk finally dimmed the beauty of the wild flowers, and the now less-than-eager pioneers began to organize their camp. Hours later, after a campfire supper, everyone was tucked snugly into sleeping bags. Gradually the chattering quieted down and gave way to the sounds of the rippling, bubbling water over the rocks in the nearby streams. The smell of the damp soil and the feel of the spongy carpet of pine needles on the ground as we made that final adjustment of body to earth and settled down for the night to look into the starry heavens awakened a sense of greatness and majesty. It was in the quiet of the night that many young girls began to experience their surroundings for the first time—not just with their eyes and ears and nose, but with their whole soul. It is the soul that reaches out to God and feels him very near.

In such a setting, young minds are prompted to ponder more deeply and wonder about things previously overlooked. "When I consider thy heavens, the work of thy fingers, the moon and the stars, which thou hast ordained; What is man, that thou art mindful of him? and the son of man, that thou visitest him? For thou hast made him a little lower than the angels, and hast crowned him with glory and honour." (Psalm 8:3-5.)

As I lay contemplating my responsibility and opportunity to speak at the sunrise service at daybreak, I marveled at the magnitude of this perfect classroom for teaching divine principles and eternal truths. There is evidence of God in everything around us when we are out in nature. Oh, if I could just help these young girls, now sound asleep, awaken in the morning to increased reverence for this beautiful world! Someone once wrote, "Beauty is of God's making; to see it is to know him very near." This surely would be a great teaching moment to open their eyes to nature as we open our hearts to prayer.

Morning seemed to come extra early, but with the gentle prodding of a few adult leaders and forceful encouragement from the youth leaders, all was in readiness for the sunrise service. Gathered around the crackling campfire, the young women seemed to be in reverent, meditative moods as they watched the smoke escape into the cool, fresh mountain air and listened to the voices of nature. Each one seemed now to be more aware of the beauties and wonders of God's creations and the feelings of peace in these surroundings.

I began by reminding the girls that the Prophet Joseph Smith went to a secluded grove to pray, and because of the testimony he gained through prayer, he came out of the grove feeling very close to his Father in heaven.

"Let me tell you the story of a young boy who went into

the forest to hunt," I continued. "While he was there he began to think about all the things his father had taught him. Probably, for the first time, they started to really mean something, and he yearned for a deeper understanding of those things, and something strange began to happen. He said, '. . . my soul hungered; and I kneeled down before my Maker and I cried unto him in mighty prayer. . . .' (Enos 4.) He prayed all day and all night, and finally a voice came into his mind, saying, 'Enos, thy sins are forgiven thee, and thou shalt be blessed.'

"Enos was a different young man when he left the forest than when he went in. He was never the same again. We read about Enos in the Book of Mormon. Many of you in this group, after your experience in the forest, will never be the same again. For some of you, this experience will be a turning point in your life. You will know this as you hear the beautiful testimonies that will be expressed in your testimony meeting."

Finally, at the conclusion of my remarks, I made this request: "Would each one of you, sometime before returning home, find a quiet spot in nature where you can experience reverence for life all around you, and talk with your Father in heaven and share with him the things that are in your heart. He is always there, and he will hear you."

I knew that Becky, the assistant youth camp director, had prayed about many things concerning the heavy responsibilities of her assignment. Under her direction the girls had decided they would like to include some special youths, the mentally handicapped, in their camp this year. This involved many challenges. Even with careful shadow leadership from the adults, Becky shouldered these heavy responsibilities. As I observed her thoughtful expression, I wondered if her load was too heavy for her young shoulders. Following the sunrise service I was relieved to see the buoyancy of her spirit and the enthusiasm with which she took part in all the well-planned activities that make camping a precious memory.

Two weeks later, in a fast and testimony meeting, Becky stood up to add her testimony to those of other girls who had participated in this camping experience.

"I was awfully worried about many things," she said,

"especially about making sure each girl was happy and no one was left out. But something about the feelings I had that special morning made me want to be alone for a while. I did as Sister Kapp suggested, and found a private spot where there was a little opening in the trees. When I knelt down on the ground, thick with pine needles, I didn't know for sure what to say, so I closed my eyes and said, 'Heavenly Father, do you know I am here?' I waited and waited, and I could hear the wind in the trees. Then I opened my eyes and saw the sun coming through the leaves, and I felt all warm inside."

She paused a moment and then, in a reverent whisper, added, "You may not think it was anything, but I know he knew I was there."

Chapter Eleven

Yes, Girls,
You Are Old Enough

C an they really do it?"
"Aren't they awfully young?" "They've had so little
experience."

While some question and wonder, those who have the
privilege of seeing young people strive to do their best express
genuine confidence and trust in a chosen generation.

Yes, girls, you are old enough. According to his promise,
the Lord will bless you young people as you prepare
yourselves to receive inspiration and revelation concerning
your duties and responsibilities in the youth organizations of
the Church.

Sandy, a young Laurel president (young in years but wise
in understanding), explained it this way: "My prayers have
changed because I have a lot of important decisions to make
now. I've got to be close to my Heavenly Father. It's an
awesome responsibility because it is so important in my life
and other girls' lives. I'm making a stronger effort to get close
to the Lord. It's not a duty but a privilege. I'm not only praying for myself, but for other people too."

In another area of the Church the youth from several
wards were meeting together. The hour was late, and many
sweet and moving testimonies had been shared when Bishop
Rogers signaled to the young priest who was conducting to
bring the meeting to a close, even though the bench was still
filled with youths eager to bear their testimonies. But having
waited this long for courage to stand, and being next in line,
Melanie could not pass this opportunity to tell "how it
works." She moved quickly to the pulpit.

"I was called to be a class president of seventeen girls," she began, "and the bishop said I was responsible for them. I was scared to death. I didn't even know for sure who they were. Then he told me to decide on my counselors and to pray and ask the Lord. I wondered how it worked—how would I know whom the Lord wanted."

For a moment she paused, shifting from one foot to the other. Then she stood erect, leaned forward, and, with conviction, said in a choked voice, "I wrote seventeen names on a piece of paper. Then I prayed about those names. Each time I would finish my prayer, I felt right about crossing off one or two names from the list. I kept thinking and praying and trying to decide until the third day. With only two names remaining, I had a strong feeling that I knew whom Heavenly Father wanted. That's how it works."

Now she continued in an enthusiastic tone. "I love these girls, and we're going to try to be good examples and reach every girl in our class so we won't lose a single one."

From where I sat I could look into the faces of the youth and I, too, could see whom the Lord had desired to be counselors to Melanie. Two girls sitting together, with smiles of confidence and eyes brimming with tears, convinced me they "won't lose a single one."

Yes, you're old enough to witness the power of the Holy Ghost when you seek inspiration from a loving Father in heaven concerning the call you have received from him through your bishop.

"But, behold, I say unto you, that you must study it out in your mind; then you must ask me if it be right, and if it is right I will cause that your bosom shall burn within you; therefore, you shall feel that it is right." (D&C 9:8.)

With a witness and a confirmation in your soul, having received inspiration, you can be an instrument in the Lord's hands in fulfilling your call as you seek to reach every single child of God for whom you have stewardship.

Ilene is a counselor in another ward. She puts it this way: "As a counselor I need to be an example in all areas. If I'm not an example, I let myself down as well as the girls. If Julie, our president, can't make a decision, I can pray about it with her; it's so much responsibility for one person."

LeeAnn, blonde and bashful but willing to share her feelings, explains, "I'm a class member. I haven't had too many assignments, but it makes a person feel needed to be involved. If we're given responsibility, we know that our leaders have confidence in us. When I get an assignment I can grow if I rely on the Lord's help. We had a couple of inactive girls, and now they're coming to our meetings. It really makes us feel good. I want them to grow as I grow. I genuinely want them to come."

The telephone rang and another experience was shared. "I know it's late, but I couldn't wait to tell you." It was the voice of Sister Byrn from a branch with few members.

"I knew it would be a good experience," she said, "but I had no idea how wonderful. You see, Marty has been a girl with some serious problems and is now a class president. I was anxious to provide every opportunity possible for her to experience the gospel in action. We discussed matters of concern that we both shared and then knelt in prayer together. We discussed the situation further, and before separating we knelt again, and this time Marty spoke to the Lord in our behalf. Together we whispered amen. Marty's eyes got big, and in a humble but excited whisper she said, 'Sister Byrn, I've never felt like this before. I know that Heavenly Father listens to prayers.'

"Oh, I love these youth." Sister Byrn's voice showed evidence of this. "They are responsible, and the Lord is working through them as we, their leaders, help them to understand their responsibilities."

So might every youth shouldering weighty responsibilities in this day say, as did Nephi of old, "I will go and do the things which the Lord hath commanded, for I know that the Lord giveth no commandments unto the children of men, save he shall prepare a way for them that they may accomplish the thing which he commandeth them." (1 Nephi 3:7.)

I bear testimony that the Lord has spoken through his prophet in this day concerning this chosen generation of youth. As you seek divine guidance concerning your responsibilities you will be used as instruments in the Lord's hands to accomplish his purposes. Yes, girls, you are old enough.

Chapter Twelve

The Greatest Lesson

*H*ow do you diplomatically encourage the boys you like and discourage those you do not want to encourage?"

That was the question I was asked to answer for the *New Era*. After deliberating for some time and praying that I might be guided in my words to the girls of the Church, I finally submitted the following response:

If I were sitting at your side and we were just chatting as friends, I would respond by asking you how you can be sure that the boy you want to discourage this week may not be the very one you wish to encourage next week. It does happen, you know. And knowing this makes the challenge considerably more difficult.

The safe approach and the one most rewarding is to develop the habit of genuine friendship with all those with whom you associate, the likable as well as those who seem to be less likable. Emotions at times interfere with clear thinking, and some likable characteristics, when carefully considered, may turn out to be only superficial, while a young man with less obvious virtues may be in the process of becoming a real prince charming, with all the attributes, characteristics, and potential that you have dreamed of.

You might remember the wisdom expressed in *The Little Prince* by Antoine de Saint-Exupéry: "Well, I must endure the presence of two or three caterpillars if I wish to become more acquainted with the butterflies." The tendency to be shortsighted may cause you to see only caterpillars when a butterfly is in the making.

Close association with a young man whose standards are unacceptable must not be encouraged, but as you maintain unwavering standards of your own, you can still reach out with friendship to all, being mindful, as someone said, that you must be on higher ground if you are to lift another.

In Doctrine and Covenants 88:40 we read: "For intelligence cleaveth unto intelligence; wisdom receiveth wisdom; truth embraceth truth; virtue loveth virtue; light cleaveth unto light; mercy hath compassion on mercy and claimeth her own. . . ."

It would seem to follow that to encourage the best, one must strive to be the best, since like spirits attract. However, boys whom you may not choose as close friends can still be lifted by your influence when you treat them with respect. Your attempt to discourage someone who would like to be a friend may be interpreted as rejection and cause him to think less of himself. When this occurs, you deprive him as well as yourself of an opportunity to lift another.

And so I would caution you about singling out those boys you want to discourage; rather, be friendly and respectful of everyone with whom you associate.

And now about that special boy you'd really like to encourage. Keep cool! A candle that burns too fast soon burns out. Be friendly. It is easier for a boy to take some initiative if you show interest and ask questions about a game he plays, a committee he serves on, or a class he's taking. He will appreciate your sincere interest, if it is not overdone, and it will be much easier to become better acquainted.

Avoid becoming too anxious about dating. A survey shows that over half the girls who graduate from high school have never had a date. You may be one of these. But the number of dates need not determine your happiness. There are many wonderful things you can be doing rather than just waiting for a date, or for your fairy godmother as Cinderella did. Just learning to enjoy people and develop friends can be exciting if you'll let it. A girl who has many friends seems to be the one who attracts even more, and as you enlarge your circle of friends, others will be drawn in. While you may not be dating, you will be sharing experiences, building memories, and having fun.

45

As you become anxious at times, and even impatient, remember to talk with your Father in heaven. Express the yearnings of your heart and seek direction. "Search diligently, pray always, and be believing, and all things shall work together for your good, if ye walk uprightly. . . ." (D&C 90:24.)

The following is an account of a young girl who grew up in a small rural community with limited educational opportunities. The first day of her senior year she found herself without friends, entering the high school in what seemed to her to be a big city. Having lost her way, she arrived late. Her anxiety was intensified when she observed that she not only didn't know her way around, but her clothing also was different, and she felt different in a most uncomfortable way.

At the close of that day, and the following morning, and each day thereafter, she poured out the yearnings of her heart to her Father in heaven, pleading for the ability to be the kind of a person worthy of friends—lots of friends, boy friends and girl friends—and promising to endeavor to keep all the commandments in return.

Days and weeks went by. Fall gave way to winter, and while friendships were forming through her sincere respect for each student, still there was a need unfulfilled. Then one Sunday afternoon what seemed like an answer to her prayer came. The telephone rang, and one of the special boys at school extended an invitation to her to attend a movie on Sunday. Oh, the yearning, the prayers, the promises, the excitement, the conflict, and now the decision. Could this be an answer to her prayers—a Sunday movie? The decision was quickly but painfully made; the invitation was declined, the response cheerful but final. Would he ever call again?

A young girl poured out the yearnings of her heart to her Father in heaven, obeyed his commandments, and trusted in the outcome. That particular young man never called again, but in due time her prayers were answered with many friends, boy friends and girl friends, and as that school year drew to a close, she was nominated by the student body to receive a special award for friendliness. Many lessons had been learned that year, but the lesson of greatest importance she expressed in these words:

"Our Father in heaven loves us.
He knows how we feel.
He listens to the yearnings of our heart.
He strengthens us when we're discouraged.
And he rewards us—in due time."

This same lesson may be yours as you "search diligently, pray always, and be believing," knowing that your Father in heaven loves you and will guide you when you strive to encourage the boys you like and extend friendship to people everywhere.

Chapter Thirteen

Tithing in Full

"Is the bishop there?" The voice on the other end of the line was breathless and anxious as I answered the phone on the first ring.

Since her tone indicated such urgency, I hesitated to explain that the bishop wasn't in just then, but she quickly interrupted my explanation. "How long before he'll be there?" she asked.

I found myself speaking rapidly as I too caught her excitement. I quickly explained that he had been called to a neighbor's home for a few minutes and should be right back. "Good," she said. "I'll come and wait."

I didn't recognize the voice, and before I could say another word, I heard the click of the receiver in my ear.

It was a beautiful May afternoon. All day I could hear the shrill voices of youth mingled occasionally with the rhythmic beating of the drums of the marching band at the high school just a few blocks away. The happy sounds announcing the culmination of another school year had kept me moving through my housework at a steady pace all day. Now I carefully put the final touches on the living room carpet, making sure the nap all went the same way. Then, standing in the doorway to avoid leaving footprints in the carpet, I admired the sprig of apricot blossoms I had placed on the mantel.

Just then the doorbell rang. Before I could answer it, Julie, a senior at the high school, came bounding into the living room and made a direct landing on the green and white loveseat near the window. I followed right behind her with no concern for the footprints in the carpet.

She was talking excitedly as she came in, and said something about having run five blocks up the hill. She was so out of breath it was impossible to make sense of what she was trying to say. She was clutching a handful of dollar bills. Then she emptied the contents of her little bag and one-dollar bills fell out everywhere, some blending into the green carpet as they landed on the floor.

Still excitedly bouncing up and down, she asked again, "When will the bishop be back?" Then, without waiting for an answer, she said, "Oh, I'll tell you," and she began her story in detail. Just before she finished, the bishop returned and quietly took a seat. Without pausing, Julie began again from the beginning to relate her story, but this time her excitement seemed a bit more subdued.

She explained how she had been working three jobs while going to school, in hopes of raising enough money to go to college in the fall. Because of many unexpected expenses, she had somehow slipped behind on her tithing. This had given her considerable concern, because she knew the importance of tithing and somehow had to make it up.

As she shifted to a different position, she told about the most exciting thing that had happened at school that day. Every member of the senior class had secretly hoped they would be selected to receive a fifty-dollar cash award or an old car that the entire student body had been admiring. Julie explained how the very thought of fifty dollars struck a responsive chord with her, since that was the exact amount required to bring her tithing up to date. She told of having a strong feeling to say a silent prayer and to promise that if she should receive the award, she would take the money and give it to the bishop for tithing just as soon as she could.

At this point Julie's voice took on a more serious tone. Her name had been announced, and she was called up to receive the award. Then the struggle began. Immediately all of her friends gathered around to share her excitement and give counsel. Of course she should take the car, they seemed to agree. One of the boys who really mattered to her said, "You've got to take the car. You can sell it for more than fifty dollars." A chorus of friends joined in, telling her that the only right thing to do was to take the car.

It was that statement, "the only right thing to do," that set her course. For Julie, there was only one right thing to do. She had already made a promise of which her friends were not aware. She must get to the bishop with the fifty dollars.

Leaving her friends somewhat bewildered, she ran to the telephone in the school office and called the information operator for the number—that would be quicker than trying to find the name in the directory.

She paused now for the first time during the full accounting, as if to say, "And here I am." Then she took a deep breath, looked directly at the bishop, and, with eyes brimming over with tears, declared, "Here's my tithing in full."

I glanced from Julie to the bishop. With a warm, sensitive expression and tears now filling his eyes, he reached for Julie's hand. Quietly I left the room, to allow for that private moment when one stands alone to give an accounting to and receive acceptance from one appointed by the power of heaven.

Half an hour passed, and I joined them again at the door as Julie was ready to leave. She was smiling now, her tear-stained face radiating an expression of victory, like one having conquered self.

"Thank you, thank you so much, bishop," she said, and the bishop replied, "I thank *you*, Julie, and your Father in heaven thanks you too."

She was half running, half skipping, as she reached the end of our sidewalk and turned north. The bishop and I stood in the doorway watching her. Just before she got out of sight, she turned and waved, then went on her happy way.

The bishop quietly closed the door, meditating aloud as he said, "The Lord's way is always a happy way."

Chapter 14

"Please Forgive Me—
I Want to Be Honest"

$\mathcal{W}$ill you please forgive me? I want to be honest," she whispered after handing me the familiar old wallet that had been taken nine years before.

With head bowed, she briefly explained that she had never stolen anything before or since. Then, as she turned to walk away, I heard a sigh of relief escape her lips.

Occasionally in a lifetime one experiences even with a stranger the reverent feeling of being in the presence of the truly pure in heart, and it was with this feeling that I fingered the old worn wallet with the broken zipper. Memories of years gone by returned to mind with the clarity of only yesterday. Snapshots of special friends along with an activity card and other identification cards gave evidence that it was indeed my old wallet. I instinctively glanced into the pocket for the paper bills and was not surprised to find what appeared to be the very same ten dollar bill that had been there the day I lost my wallet.

It had been nine years since, as a student at Brigham Young University, I had used the telephone in the Joseph Smith Building and had carelessly left my wallet in the phone booth. I returned to the lost and found department regularly for several days before finally giving up my desperate hope of ever getting my wallet and money back. That ten dollars was all the money I had, and I was in the habit of measuring my expenditures with great care. Without an understanding landlady, its loss could have caused some real problems. But that incident, like many others, faded into the background as more important memories crowded in.

Years had passed. One snowy afternoon the mailman delivered a rather fat envelope with two letters enclosed. The first one, from Mom, included a few questions about the other letter, which began:

"To whom it may concern, anyone knowing the whereabouts of Ardeth Greene please forward this letter. It is very important that contact be made as soon as possible to settle some unfinished business at the B.Y.U." A name and an address were then given.

My first reaction was of indignation, since I knew of no unfinished business for which I was responsible. When my mind flashed back to my first experience with a bank account when I had written a check for groceries on the wrong bank, I became a little less indignant and wondered what unfinished business I needed to set in order.

With some anxiety I found in the Salt Lake telephone directory the name of the person who had signed the letter. I quickly dialed the number and asked for the person by name. A pleasant voice responded, "This is she." I identified myself and began with some apologies for any unfinished business, only to be interrupted by an intense voice speaking rapidly as if to spill out all the words at once. She continued unloading her story until finally there was evidence of a burdened heart now relieved from foreign and contaminating elements too long contained.

It seemed that this young woman, now a wife and mother, had been in nurses' training at BYU. She had worked to put herself through school, but she needed an additional ten dollars for tuition, so she turned to her boy friend for help. She promised to return the loan by Friday, but when Friday came, she was still short ten dollars, in spite of her earnest prayers.

Not knowing why, she had walked into the telephone booth and found an old worn wallet. She explained how her heart started to pound, since she'd never been tempted like this before. She held her breath when she opened it to find a single ten dollar bill. Then the question: was this indeed an answer to her prayer?

She interrupted her steady flow of words to explain that since then she had learned that Satan knows when we are being tested and when we might weaken under pressure, and we can be sure he will be there if there is a chance we might fall.

Then, picking up the story again, she told of paying her boy friend, whom she later married, finishing school, and now raising a beautiful family and rejoicing in the blessings of the gospel.

Her voice choked with emotion as she painfully related the details about the old wallet. She emphasized how she had been taught right from wrong and how she was well acquainted with the principle of honesty. Her conscience had prompted her but she had listened to the wrong voice and had acted contrary to that which she knew was right. She explained how taking the money had seemed justified at the time, but for nine years her conscience had never been at peace. She told of her suffering for what she acknowledged as being a sin.

Elder Orson F. Whitney once wrote concerning sin: "Sin is the transgression of divine law, as made known through the conscience or by revelation. A man sins when he violates his conscience going contrary to light and knowledge—not the light and knowledge that has come to his neighbor, but that which has come to himself. He sins when he does the opposite of what he knows to be right."

For nine years, through many moves, the old burden had lain deeply tucked away in this young woman's dresser drawer. Though she'd considered throwing it away many times, it seemed impossible to do. There is no way one can throw away a wrong.

One day, while she was straightening the drawer, the old wallet surfaced again. This time she felt she must get rid of it, but in the right way. She had learned many valuable lessons over the years, and she had a quiet assurance that even this experience had served a purpose. She thoughtfully opened the wallet once again and examined it. This time her fingers uncovered a small orange card tucked away in a tiny compartment not previously noticed. This orange card would be the key to unloading her burden. On it was the address of a clinic in Calgary, Alberta, Canada, where a medical examination for a student's visa had been given.

With a prayer in her heart, she sent a letter to the clinic, addressed "To Whom It May Concern," and asking that it be forwarded, if possible. The letter was forwarded first to my parents in Canada and then back to Utah, where it finally reached its intended destination. Contact had been made, but the wallet was yet to be returned. During our telephone conversation she indicated the wallet would be mailed that very day.

When one sees in another a keen sense of right and wrong and a great virtue carefully tuned by the Spirit through struggle and final victory, there is a reaching out for association with that person, a desire to meet one so honest in heart. Thus I asked her if she would consider delivering the wallet in person. She seemed a little embarrassed at the request until I assured her it would be an honor and a privilege to meet a person who had such honesty of character. She agreed to meet me that afternoon at the office where I was working.

When I returned from lunch, the young woman was sitting beside my desk, with her back to me. Her shoulders were narrow but straight, and she sat erect on the edge of the chair with both feet squarely on the floor in front of her.

As I approached, she shifted nervously, then stood up. Then, as though she had rehearsed this experience in her mind a hundred times, she reached out a steady hand, looked me squarely in the eye, and handed me the wallet. Her steady gaze reflected the radiance of a good and honest life.

When she whispered, "Will you please forgive me? I want to be honest," my words would not come. I could only reach for her hand and nod affirmatively.

"Behold," the Lord has said, "he who has repented of his sins, the same is forgiven, and I, the Lord, remember them no more." (D&C 58:42.)

I went to the window and watched her turn the corner with a lilt in her step. Then, returning to my desk, I again heard the echo of her words. "Will you please forgive me? I want to be honest."

Chapter 15

Seek Ye First the Kingdom of Heaven

May I tell you about Heber, the man I married. He was raised on a farm by a widowed mother with nine children. After he completed his mission, we decided to borrow enough to get married on and begin life together—with two goals: (1) trust in the Lord, and (2) seek first the kingdom of God.

I remember our first visitor—a bill collector from a local hospital, asking for a back payment on the expenses we had assumed after the death of his mother a few months previously. In this seeming plight, we decided to set some goals, and they included his going to school and my getting a job (by the way, I had never had a job other than helping Dad on the farm irrigating and hauling hay and working in a little country grocery store). We decided to dream dreams and think big. It was kind of like a game. My husband said, "Where do you want to work?" And with all the confidence that comes in the privacy of your own little house of dreams, I said, half jokingly, "Samuels," which was at that time considered to be one of the loveliest dress shops in town. He stopped me and said, "Tomorrow you will go and apply for a job at Samuels; it will be a good experience for you." I've wondered since exactly what he meant.

My heart started to pound at the very thought of riding the bus downtown alone and maybe getting lost. Heber seemed to ignore my anxiety as he prompted me about how I was to set a goal in my mind to get a job at Samuels and to go in with confidence. Mind you, being the farm boy that he was and acquainted with poverty, he didn't have much to spare.

The next day as I walked past the beautifully decorated windows with such high-fashioned clothing and I looked down at my homespun dress, my heart sank and my courage departed completely. I hurried to the other side of the street, where the challenge seemed a little less threatening. But even there it was too much. I looked down the street to the dime store and thought, I could go there and tell my husband there was no opening at Samuels. But how could I carry the burden of a lie because I was too scared? After crossing the street twice more I faced the store from the other side of the street and finally just walked across the street and went through the front door of Samuels without stopping—trusting in the Lord for courage, but my goal was to say my speech and get out.

The store was empty of customers. It was early in the morning, and to the first gentleman I saw I nervously gave my speech: "I'm impressed with your store. I know how to work hard and I know I can sell your merchandise." (Under my breath, I added, "Now let me go.")

Mr. Roden, who was dressed in a gray flannel suit, stepped back and with a half-smile under his very proper mustache said, "You don't say! Come with me." In the manager's office he said to a very dignified-looking gentleman, "This young lady says she can sell our merchandise." I've never yet been able to interpret their smiles but Mr. Dye said, "Would you like to begin Monday?" I could hardly wait to tell Heber.

We trusted in the Lord. We dreamed a dream and set a goal. And we both got through school.

Then we dared to dream of having a home, a lovely home, so we set a goal. With no money and no experience in building, but with trust and faith and a specific goal, we began first on paper. We knew nothing about blueprints, but eventually we drew our own plans; then, without the finances to build, the whole idea became an obsession to us, so we built a model to scale from scraps. We set a goal to have a house in two years and build it ourselves. We bought a lot in a beautiful area and we walked across it in the morning, in the evening, in the wind, in the rain, in the fall, and in the winter, and then came the spring.

Heber was called to the high council, and he explained to

Elder Spencer W. Kimball, who was the visiting authority at stake conference, that we planned to build in just one month outside the stake. Elder Kimball just said, "We'll call you, and it will work out." At the end of the month we went to the stake president and explained that we were ready to build and wondered about a release. He said, "You talk to the Lord about that; it was he who called you." So we went home and talked to the Lord; then we sold the lot. Still, within two years, we had built our home on a more ideal location than we had thought possible within the stake, and had furnished it elegantly. The day the carpet layers finished I sat in the middle of the floor hugging the scraps, with tears rolling down my cheeks. "Seek ye first the kingdom of God, and all else shall be added."

And now as I stand about halfway between my horizons, my knowledge of the past assures me without question, with a testimony and a witness, that my horizon yet ahead is as great as the goals I set for myself, if I make myself work toward them.

Chapter 16

A Treasured Christmas

The late harvest that year was followed by an early frost, and many of the crops were under a blanket of snow.

As Christmas approached, we children played the wishing game in the Eaton's catalog until the toy section was well marked by the curled edges of the pages. We tried hard to limit our long list of wants to a few special items, knowing that we must be selective since Mom and Dad had to pay Santa for his Christmas treasures. But after a family council to consider a serious matter, our choices were easily made.

Brian, our twelve-year-old crippled cousin who had just been ordained a deacon, was more anxious than ever to walk, and if enough money could be raised, it was possible that the Mayo Clinic in Minnesota could help him. This would require a great sacrifice, but the choice was ours. We could each make our own decision and, if we chose, we could request that the money for our Christmas be given to Brian in hopes of providing medical attention that would allow him to abandon the wheelchair we had all taken turns pushing so often. The Eaton's catalog got lost somewhere in the shuffle as we each talked with great anticipation of our part in helping Brian.

Christmas Eve came and with it the children's party at the church. I remember being a little disappointed that Santa wore his shabby old suit to our party, but Mom explained that he kept his good one to wear when he came later that night to make his official visit, and that seemed like a good idea to me.

Christmas Eve found cousins, aunts, and uncles all at Mamma Leavitt's big two-story house (she was such a special grandmother that we all called her Mamma Leavitt), and there in her home twenty-one children were tucked into beds of some sort—after hanging up twenty-one stockings.

Even as a child I remember that the air was filled with gaiety and smiles radiated from the faces of young and old.

The next morning our socks were bulging with goodies. Old dolls had beautiful new wardrobes that Santa had skillfully prepared, and old toys had new paint, and Brian was going to the Mayo Clinic.

It didn't take long to tidy things up since there were very few wrappings, but that was good, because we had exciting things planned with our fathers while our mothers were busy getting ready for the big dinner. The second best turkey in Dad's flock was roasting in the oven and filling the air with that Christmas dinner smell, while the very finest turkey had been selected to go into the big box along with homemade pies, jams, jellies, fruits, and vegetables. On top was a handmade apron carefully wrapped in a piece of soft white tissue paper and tied with a bit of ribbon that had served that same purpose many times before.

Each of us, all bundled up, was lifted onto the big wagon along with the box of goodies and away we went through the deep snow, listening to the steady rhythm of the horses' hooves until we reached the river about three miles away, where Mr. and Mrs. Opstall lived in their little log house.

The Opstalls were an elderly couple from Belgium who had once been wealthy but who had sold all their earthly possessions to flee to freedom in Canada. As we jumped off the wagon into the crunchy snow, we each waited eagerly to be given one of the items from the big box. My brother got to carry the turkey and I carried one of Mamma Leavitt's delicious mincemeat pies. It was quite a job trudging through the deep snow, trying to follow in Dad's big steps with our arms loaded.

Inside the one-room home, the bare floors were warmed by a glowing fire, and the long slab table in the middle of the room was gradually piled higher and higher as we each presented our expression of love.

The Opstalls couldn't speak a word of English, but I remember thinking that I knew exactly what they were telling us. The words didn't really seem to make any difference, but I was puzzled by their tears when they seemed so happy, and I recall Mom trying to explain this to me later. It didn't make much sense, but as long as they were happy, I guessed it was okay if they wanted to cry.

I'll never forget sitting down to the big dinner with a special place for everyone, including Brian in his wheelchair at the corner of the table because it seemed to fit better there. And down at the far end Papa Leavitt bowed his head and gave a prayer that lasted ever so long.

That night we all got to stay up late, and we sat around in the big living room with our moms and dads and talked about things. After our family prayer, when I was tucked into bed, indelibly imprinted on my mind was the lesson that Christmas is an excited, good feeling inside, and how I wished every Christmas might be like this one!

Chapter 17

The Influence of a
Young Woman

It was Sunday afternoon, and the chapel was already filled. The sound of extra folding chairs being set up in the cultural hall could be heard above the prelude music. Many friends and family members had come from far and near to rejoice with Elder Thorne in his sacred call from a prophet of the Lord, a call to serve in Argentina for two years as a special witness for Christ.

Just before the music stopped, Elder Thorne and his parents left the door where they had been shaking hands and made their way to the stand. All eyes were on them as they took their seats just behind the pulpit. It was easy from where I sat to look over the congregation and locate the missionary's proud grandparents. This was a special event for the entire family, and they were all a part of it. His four younger brothers were smiling, probably because they would get to expand into his room as soon as he entered the mission home, or maybe because they were anticipating how they would feel in just a few short years when they would respond to the call of a prophet.

I observed in the large audience an unusual number of young women, many of them visitors to our ward. How could this be? Certainly they were not all assuming to be Elder Thorne's girl friends, were they?

These young women brought with them excitement and enthusiasm, and their very presence added to the beauty and importance of the occasion. Among them I spotted the plain, the confident, the bashful, but common to each was the radiant, youthful expression of anticipation and commitment.

I studied the expressions on the faces of several of these girls and then followed their gaze to Elder Thorne, in dark suit, white shirt with conservative tie, and a little-shorter-than-usual haircut.

The young men and young women in the audience represented a circle of friends bursting with pride and sharing the honor of one of their number. It was not hard to believe that in the heart of each one were the words of the song, "I'll go where you want me to go, dear Lord, . . . I'll do what you want me to do."

Since the girls were sitting in groups of twos and threes and fours, it appeared evident they were not competitors seeking his attention, but that they too were part of the Church's missionary effort. But what part did they play? What had their influence been in Elder Thorne's preparation?

In the closing remarks of this young man, who was spiritually mature beyond his years, one began to sense the powerful influence of his friends. After expressing gratitude for family and loved ones, and before his final testimony, he grasped each side of the pulpit and dropped his head for just a moment. Then he looked up and quietly said, "And I give thanks to all my friends, especially you girls in the audience who have kept the standards and encouraged me to do the same." His voice deepened as he added, "Thank you for your influence, which has helped me prepare for a mission."

After the closing prayer there seemed to be a spontaneous gravitation of young men and women from all parts of the building, moving forward until they encircled their young missionary friend. Without accompaniment, their voices united in singing "God be with you till we meet again," like a prayer to heaven from the voices of living angels. The tears flowed freely from the eyes of these youth who had played a very vital part in helping to build a worthy and an able missionary.

In that moment I witnessed the power of love and support from friends that would serve as a reservoir of strength to each one of them in the days to come.

Leaving the chapel, I was driven by the desire to understand more fully how those young women had played such a powerful role in the missionary's preparation. If their role could be identified, perhaps it could be repeated over and over with immeasurable results. My search for answers led me to many youths in many areas. The first responses were stated in a variety of ways but always the same message: "We don't know what it is, but we can tell you what it isn't."

Tim said, "It isn't just telling me that I ought to go on a mission, because I want to make that decision myself." After a few moments of contemplation, David looked thoughtful and said, "Some girls say they won't go with you if you don't plan on going on a mission. It doesn't seem to matter to them whether you are a good missionary or not, and that's no help."

Brent added, "A girl can talk to you about a mission, but when she starts to get close to you and influences you the wrong way, it is not what she says that counts."

Bradley added, "A girl has a lot of power, and if you like her, you try to do the things that impress her. If good things impress her, then that is what you try to do."

In a tone of conviction David said, "Some girls don't even care if you go on a mission or not. I think they should care but shouldn't try to force you, because when you are forced to do something, you just want to turn and go the other way. You want to use your own agency about something that important."

It was Ross who said, "Occasionally, I get the idea a girl is more concerned about what I ought to be doing than what she ought to be doing."

Stan added, "If a girl is not willing to pay the price to do what she ought to be doing, then I think she is a hypocrite to be trying to tell me that I should go on a mission."

Finally, all of the comments about what it isn't were expressed. Then, like nuggets of wisdom, I learned from many young men those truths which, when understood and practiced by the young women of the Church, can be an influence of such power and magnitude as to affect for good every corner of the Church and the entire world.

Young women of The Church of Jesus Christ of Latter-day Saints, can the young men with whom you associate know that you have a standard of excellence from which you will not depart? Can they know by what you say and do that you honor and respect your parents and that you follow the counsel of the leaders of the Church? Can they know that you will delay dating until after you are sixteen because a prophet of the Lord has given that direction? By your actions, can they know that you have made up your mind to be good, and you will not weaken? Can they look to your friendship to gain confidence and respect for themselves? Will your language, your dress, your choice of entertainment, music, books, and movies help the young men who associate with you develop admiration and respect for womanhood? As young men are exposed to the world's distorted role of womanhood, can they see in you the refinement and sweetness that encourages an attitude of reverence, respect, and honor for that sacred calling?

Strange that I had not realized before that it is not when a young woman encourages a young man to go on a mission that her greatest influence is felt; rather, it is when, by her actions, she reveals her commitment and testimony to the gospel of Jesus Christ and gives evidence of it through her power and influence in the advancement of good.

When a young man is encouraged by the example and testimony of his friends to do those things which magnify his priesthood, preparation for a mission becomes a top priority in his life. Following his mission he is even better prepared for the responsibilities awaiting him as he continues to serve in the kingdom.

As a young woman begins to comprehend and accept her responsibility to her own mission in life, she becomes a powerful influence in the lives of the young men who associate with her. As she begins to prepare for her ultimate destiny, they are encouraged by her example to attain their own goals.

A faithful young Latter-day Saint woman will strive to be apart from the world, will resist the enticements of the world and plan carefully according to God's will concerning her. As she seeks to understand her mission, she will come to realize her vital role in building the kingdom of God.

It takes mighty souls to fill the great mission of womanhood and to prepare in due time to be mothers and wives and raise up a seed unto the Lord. That is why these precious preparation years of youth are so vitally, so desperately, so urgently needed, and why they must be handled and guarded with care. If the preparation is cut short by early dating or misused by neglect or interrupted by early marriage, or if disobedience or lack of control comes into place, these matters are of eternal consequence, for they affect generations yet unborn.

A young woman's influence is determined by how she chooses to use this special time for preparation. She can clutter it with nonessentials or she can be about the work and mission of womanhood and strengthen her friends along the way.

Her mission, her destiny, her course in life are to develop those virtues, attributes, characteristics and qualities, talents and skills, intellectual pursuits and spiritual promptings that enrich the lives of others. She must develop a spiritual reservoir from which all members of her family may draw strength. She must contribute to an environment where God will find boys and girls, men and women to accomplish his purposes.

Young women who are filling their own lives with righteousness, who are developing a taste for all that is good and wholesome, who are learning skills for successful womanhood and motherhood, radiate the light of God. Young men feel this light when they are in the presence of noble young women. The nobility within them is awakened. A yearning to be worthy of being the eternal companion of a noble daughter of God is kindled. Young men will stretch their lives to be equal to the greatness of the soul they feel within themselves. A mission is one of the initial steps that can result from the influence of a young woman whose own preparation causes her to radiate the light of God.

"That which is of God is light; and he that receiveth light, and continueth in God, receiveth more light; and that light groweth brighter and brighter until the perfect day." (D&C 50:24.)

When a young man returns home from his mission, he should feel assured that the young woman at home has kept pace with him spiritually, is prepared to receive inspiration, has progressed intellectually and socially, and is ready in every way to stand as an eternal companion to sustain him, not drain him. Then, together, they are ready to accept the further responsibilities the Lord has for those who love him and keep his commandments.

It was Sunday again, and another worthy missionary was responding to the call. I chanced my frequently asked question one more time, and Elder Snow, glancing warmly and respectfully at the young girl standing by his side, smiled and responded, "She never told me I should go on a mission. I just always knew it was important to her because everything about the Church is important to Jannie."

Chapter Eighteen

"You're Like a Mother"

The stake president sent me to you; he said you'd understand since you don't have any children either." The woman's tone of voice revealed an attitude of resentment as she stood at my front door, and although we were strangers at that moment, I recognized her seeming resentment as a coverup for a troubled and anguished heart. During the several hours that followed, her concerns were spilled out, baring her soul, and her tears flowed freely while she spoke of blessings denied.

She came as a stranger, but sharing deeply personal concerns made us sisters, and I gave silent thanks for the inspiration of the stake president who directed her to my door. Upon leaving she turned, and there was a brief moment of silence as our eyes met; then in a tone of gratitude she said, "The stake president was right, you do understand. Thank you."

As she drove away, I rejoiced in the blessing of being able to ease the burden of another, for I did understand. And as I watched her car turn the corner out of sight I was reminded of the words of Elder Neal A. Maxwell at a Brigham Young University fireside: "Every time we navigate safely on this great and narrow way there are other ships that are nearly lost or which are lost which can find their way because of our light."

My path to understanding had not always been one of light; in fact, on occasion there had been much darkness.

As BYU Professor Bruce C. Hafen had once stated: "There are conditions of uncertainty, difficulty, temptations, and insecurity—and yet, they are the very fabric that gives mortality its profound meaning. For only under such conditions is it possible for man to reach enough, search enough, and yearn enough for real growth of the spirit to be possible." But it is possible, and yet there were times over the past years that I really wondered.

I remember a Sunday morning some years ago. Sunday School was a time for rejoicing except on Mother's Day. But I had told myself it would be different this year. The organ music was playing softly as young girls moved quietly down the aisle passing small plants along each row to the mothers who were standing. Last year it was geraniums, this year begonias, and this year I vowed that I would be braver than all the years before. But as the mothers one by one received their small tribute and the girls approached my row, those old familiar feelings returned, and I wished I hadn't come to Sunday School, at least not on Mother's Day.

The little pots in silver wrapping were passed along each row until all the mothers were seated and then, as before, one more plant was passed. And once again I heard the usual whisper, "Go ahead, you deserve it. It's OK, we've got plenty," and then forcing the little plant into my tightened fist someone whispered, "You're like a mother!"

The meeting ended and my escape through the cultural hall to the back door seemed blocked with unidentifiable objects. I must not cry, I must set a good example, I told myself, especially since my husband was in the chapel carrying out the responsibilities according to his call, showing such genuine concern for others and never thinking of himself. But how could I forget myself when the pounding in my ears, "You're like a mother," seemed to mock the beating of my heart, as my hands resisted the weight of the little begonia.

This year was no different. I thought of the saying "time heals all things," but years were passing and there was no healing, only anguish and heartache. My mind flooded with questions asked too frequently. Were not my eternal companion and I commanded in our sacred temple ceremony to multiply and replenish the earth and to have joy in our posterity? Was there to be no posterity? No joy?

My steps quickened as I hurried to the safety of my own

home just a few blocks from the chapel. But even there I found loneliness as I tried to ignore the dinner table set with love and care, but with only two plates.

Another day and I would need to try again, even harder. Weeks later the doorbell rang and a little lad new to the neighborhood looked up with eager eyes, asking, "Can your kids come out and play?" A coldness seemed to creep over me and I almost whispered so no one could hear, "I don't have any." The child in a somewhat questioning tone asked, "Aren't you a mother?" With a quick and somewhat abrupt response my voice replied, "No, I'm not." The little boy's eyes squinted, and with his head cocked to one side in the innocence of childhood, he asked the question that I had never dared to put into words: "If you're not a mother, what are you?"

Behind the closed door with my back against the wall my whole soul cried out, "Dear God, if I'm not a mother, what am I?" And again the searching question—what was the divine plan for my husband and me and what would the Lord have us do?

Several of our closest and dearest friends had adopted children who had brought the joy of parenthood to their lives. These precious children were in fact their very own through the sealing power of the Holy Priesthood, sealed in an eternal family unit. Together we continued inquiring of the Lord through prayer and fasting and seeking divine guidance as spoken of in Doctrine and Covenants 9:8-9:

"But, behold, I say unto you, that you must study it out in your mind; then you must ask me if it be right, and if it is right I will cause that your bosom shall burn within you; therefore, you shall feel that it is right.

"But if it be not right you shall have no such feelings, but you shall have a stupor of thought. . . ."

But why the stupor of thought when we yearned so for that burning in the bosom, that quiet confirmation that gives assurance of the Lord's will?

We struggled with the desire to experience increased faith that we might receive a positive response to our desired decision, but in our minds we could hear the words, "Whatsoever ye ask the Father in my name it shall be given unto you, that is expedient for you. And if ye ask anything that is not expedient for you, it shall turn unto your condemnation." (D&C 88:64-65.)

Oh, that we might know the Lord's will concerning us!

Like a bird flying through turbulent winds, there were many highs and lows during the coming years and finally, perhaps because of a readiness to receive, the message came. "Trust in the Lord with all thine heart; and lean not unto thine own understanding. In all thy ways acknowledge him, and he shall direct thy paths." (Proverbs 3:5-6.) The words were not new but the message came as an answer to a fervent prayer. "Trust in the Lord." Surely this was the key.

Almost with excitement thoughts came flooding to my mind. Faith in the Lord Jesus Christ—was this not the first principle of the gospel? Faith in a loving father, a divine purpose, an eternal plan. Faith that all things shall come to pass in the due time of the Lord.

I waited anxiously to share these feelings with Heber. I always waited up until he returned from his meetings, even on late nights, because that sharing time had become so special. In a home where a faithful, obedient servant of the Lord endowed with the Holy Priesthood of God honors his priesthood and magnifies his calling, there is a reservoir of limitless power from which to draw strength. This night I would ask for another blessing at the hands of my eternal companion through whom God would speak. And with increased faith we would know God's will concerning us.

Heber had a way of sensing when I needed to talk, and when he arrived home he knew this was one of those times. As we shared our feelings, the quiet hours passed until only the embers were left glowing in the fireplace. Since we had entered into the patriarchal order of celestial marriage, it was possible for a blessing to be pronounced through the power and authority of the priesthood by the natural patriarch in our home. There was a bridge spanned between heaven and earth through priesthood channels, and never again would there be that seeming unquenchable thirst, for we had partaken of living waters.

Guided by this noble man and inspired by the Lord, together we found the direction that would become our purpose for life. We recalled the words of President McKay as we remembered them—the noblest aim in life is to strive to make other lives happy, and then, drawing from the never-ending strength of a righteous companion, I listened to his counsel. "You need not possess children to love them. Loving is not synonymous with possessing, and possessing is not necessarily loving. The world is filled with people to be loved, guided, taught, lifted, and inspired."

And finally, together we reread the words of the prophet Joseph Fielding Smith: "If any worthy person is denied in this life the blessings which so readily come to others, and yet lives faithfully and to the best of his or her ability in striving to keep the commandments of the Lord, then nothing will be lost to him. Such a person will be given all the blessings that can be given. The Lord will make up to him the fulness after this life is ended and the full life has come. The Lord will not overlook a single soul who is worthy, but will grant to him all that can be given. . . ." (*Doctrines of Salvation,* Bookcraft, 1955, 2:176-77.)

I didn't hear Heber's final words as he quietly closed the book; my soul was at peace in slumber, with my head resting on his shoulder.

Things were never quite the same after that. From this source of strength came a quiet peace like the rising of the sun when the warmth of its rays moves upward until it encompasses the entire sky and there are no clouds of darkness in any direction.

This eternal union would be preserved and we would grow toward perfection together as we made a vow to trust in the Lord and his timing knowing "all that my Father hath shall be given unto him." (D&C 84:38.) There would still be questions, but there would also be answers. What do we do in the meantime and what is the purpose of life were the questions I asked the patriarch in our home.

I cannot recall just when it happened, but our cookie jar was just not large enough to contain all the cookies that were dispensed from our door in one day. And so it became a cookie drawer, familiar to the entire neighborhood, young and old. Even the sixteen- and seventeen-year-olds would come, using the excuse, "We need a cookie," in hopes Heber was home with time to listen to them, have fun, and "throw in" a little "fatherly advice," as they called it.

On one occasion when a private conversation seemed to last for hours, I questioned Heber's priorities as they related to a previously planned seemingly important schedule. He nodded his head in understanding of my concern, then thoughtfully responded, "Is anything of greater priority than a young man's life?" I learned never to question his priorities.

My rewards for waiting came at many unexpected times, such as at the grocery store, when the boy bagging my groceries very spontaneously said, "Your husband is a great guy to talk to."

A letter to him from a grateful mother: "Thanks for talking to my boy—it has made all the difference. It's hard without a dad, and now he's decided he wants to go on a mission. Thank you for the time you spend with my son."

One day a little boy brushed past me at the kitchen door, coached by a friend who led the way. "Bradly sez ya get one in both hands," was the comment as his more experienced companion eagerly pulled the cookie drawer wide open for a careful selection. With a concealed smile I responded, "Bradley's right." Once their choice was made, the little scavengers bounded from the door with their treasures, and as I stood watching, my heart rejoiced.

A small miracle was beginning to take place. ". . . I give unto men weakness that they may be humble; and my grace is sufficient for all men that humble themselves before me; for if they humble themselves before me, and have faith in me, then will I make weak things become strong unto them." (Ether 12:27.)

An eternal union can be strengthened through seeming adversity, and disappointment can be the foundation for eternal bonds of love and bind a companionship against all the threatening powers that beset the lives of mortals.

Blessings are not denied but sometimes delayed, and it is only in matters of great consequence that souls are bound close together as they reach upward to God. And he is there—" . . . lo, I am with you alway, even unto the end of the world. . . ." (Matthew 28:20.)

Years passed swiftly, bringing fulfillment of carefully laid plans as we shared in the joy of seeing the sons of our friends leave for missions and daughters planning for temple marriage and, eventually, that special excitement reserved only for grandparents. While Heber became a power of unwavering strength, on occasion I would experience a fleeting yearning that would each time be quietly softened. At such a time a kind Father in heaven who knows and understands all things put into the mouth of one of his appointed servants during a setting apart blessing those words that would reconfirm and bring to our hearts that "peace that passeth all understanding."

Through the years we have been blessed with boundless opportunities for growth and development—opportunities to serve our fellowmen, young and old, and to rejoice in the gift of life; to see God's handiwork in all that is good; to love deeply and grow spiritually; and to strive to make other lives happy.

It was the week following Mother's Day when, sorting through the mail, I recognized the California return address and rejoiced in another letter from "one of my girls," usually an announcement of an important event, maybe a new little baby. But the message was different this time, like the answer to a long-forgotten prayer:

"I would like to share with you some of the feelings I have at this Mother's Day time. When I was a small girl I can remember other Mother's Days—the passing out of carnations to the mothers in the ward and how special it seemed. Someday I could stand too, perhaps, and be honored along with the rest. This Mother's Day came with special meaning to me as my mind reflected back on a sweet but frail ninety-six-year-old grandmother, the sacrifices and love of my own mother, a sweet mother-in-law who always listens, and now my own tiny special daughter smiling trustingly at her mother's awkward handling.

"But not only did my thoughts reflect back to mothers of blood but to a special, beautiful person who so touched my life as to make me always love and respect her as certainly a mother to me in all the special qualities that go with the word. If you could only know the number of times just thinking of you softened a hardened heart or helped me to my

73

knees when our Heavenly Father's guidance was so needed."

My heart was full to overflowing as my eyes filled with tears of gratitude and blurred my vision so I could read no further. As the tears quietly rolled down my cheeks I thought of the privilege that had been ours to touch in a meaningful way the lives of Jim, Karen, Becky, Paul, Mark, Mindy, Wanda, and many other precious souls we have loved so deeply. And then I reflected on the many lives even yet to be reached and taught, loved, and guided, and a silent prayer escaped my lips: "Thank you, dear God. Truly my cup runneth over. Thou hast allowed thy humble servant to be used as an instrument in thy hands."

With the tears brushed away, I continued reading.

"I love you so very much and I pray often that the Lord's guiding spirit may always be with you so that you can continue to bless the lives of those around you. You're like a mother to me.

Love, Cathie."

Chapter Nineteen

Bricks or Straw?

his mortal probation, this proving time, is not, I think, so much for our Father in heaven to find out how well we will do, since he already knows us anyway. Rather, it is a time for us to find out who we really are and what we are made of.

I have a little six-year-old niece, Shelly, who proudly and frequently reminds me that she is made of bricks. I would like to share with you an experience that for her became a marvelous realization, and for me, a great lesson.

This summer while she was taking a hike with her mother and father, what was intended to be a three-mile hike turned out to be a fourteen-mile hike, due to the misinterpretation of a sign and the loss of direction. After several miles, these unseasoned hikers came to a gradual halt at the crest of a little hill. While sitting down for a welcome rest, Shelly's mother determined to make the best of the situation and use it as a teaching opportunity. She explained to Shelly that this would be a chance to see if they were made of bricks or straw. The comparison had a familiar ring because of that favorite childhood story, "The Three Little Pigs." She explained that their final destination was still the camp, so that while the change of plans from three miles to fourteen miles was somewhat discouraging, it was not distressing, because they were not lost; they knew where they were going.

This sounded like an adventuresome opportunity to Shelly, and not realizing the full impact of the situation, she was anxious to end their brief rest in order to "find out what we are made of."

Like many teaching and growing opportunities, the newness and novelty soon wore off and then the real lesson and testing began. Driven by the desire to "find out what we are made of," this little six-year-old kept walking and walking. Though she welcomed the little rest periods that became more frequent as the day wore on, something within her nature would not let her give up. Sometimes she would hold her dad's hand, which was always close, and sometimes her mother's; but never did she suggest being carried or giving up.

Near the end of the day, just as the sun was setting, Shelly's face was flushed and sunburned, smudged from the frequent brush of her dusty hands across her face to get the hair out of her eyes. Her sneakers were coated with dust that had crept up past her socks and blended into the suntan on her short, tired legs. Without any complaint, and not being aware of the location of the camp, she finally stopped, exhausted, to make an accounting. Shoulders drooping and hands hanging limply at her side, she said, "Mom, I guess I'm made of straw."

At this moment her mother let go of her hand, dropped down on one knee, wrapped the little girl in her arms, and explained, "No, my dear, you are made of bricks. Our camp is in sight, and we have made it, the full fourteen miles."

Together the parents picked up this little soul who had gone as far as she could and only then had stopped to make an accounting. Their rejoicing was beyond measure as they passed the finish line into camp. Now on frequent occasions Shelly reports, with renewed confidence, "I can do it 'cause I'm made of bricks."

When we too have gone as far as we can, we can be sure the camp will be in sight, and we will feel the security of the Lord's arms enfolding us if we don't give up when the going gets tough—and it will.

Chapter Twenty

Graduation

first noticed her in the audience sitting about five rows from the front. She was wearing a blue cotton dress, and her long brown hair fell loosely around her pretty face. Almost always when one speaks to a group of young people, there are a few in the audience who by their countenance convey a readiness to hear, an anticipation for what they expect to learn. These few mold the message as the speaker reads from their countenance that which finds lodging within the soul. When one is taught by the Spirit, the words heard are usually of little consequence when compared to the message that is received. It is as though those in the audience hear more than is actually spoken and understand more than is really explained. This girl seemed to be hanging on every word.

Following the fireside I lost sight of her in the crowd until later, when I saw her blue dress out of the corner of my eye. She was standing alone, waiting. Finally she made her way toward the stand. "Do you have time to talk to me?" she asked. Her tone when she said "me" gave me cause to wonder about her self-esteem and self-confidence. She spoke only briefly as, without revealing any specific details, she indicated an inner struggle and turmoil. She then turned to leave, maybe to avoid the possibility of being pressed for further details. I wondered at the time about the burden that was being carried on such young shoulders. How might it be lifted? In my heart I felt that I would take it from her if I could.

Several days later I received a letter that began, "I don't know if you will remember me, but I was the one in the blue dress sitting in the middle about five rows back." In her letter she was able to risk a bit more as she described some of her own personal challenges. Once again I felt the urge to step in and ease her burden, if possible. She wrote, "Please send me a copy of the four keys that you talked about that worked for you." I sensed in her request a genuine desire to give the principles a try. My response to her letter included the four keys with examples of the testimony of their effectiveness.

The first key is found in Proverbs 3:5-6: "Trust in the Lord with all thine heart; and lean not unto thine own understanding. In all thy ways acknowledge him, and he shall direct thy paths."

The second key, equally important, is to believe in yourself with an understanding that you are a child of God, with Godlike attributes to be discovered and developed.

The third key is to have a worthwhile goal, one worthy of total commitment, even an obsession, to attain and know the necessary steps to achieve it.

The fourth key might be described by the experience of a child who, while trying out new roller skates, falls and skins her knee. Her immediate tears and loud crying bring her mother running to her aid. However, just as her mother arrives the little girl stops crying. When asked by her surprised mother why she has stopped so quickly, she says, "I just told myself to stop and then I made myself mind me." The fourth key is to decide what you are going to do and then determine the necessary steps to accomplish it—to make yourself mind you.

Some weeks later, another letter arrived that read, in part, "I have read your letter and the four keys over and over. They really lift my spirits when I am depressed. I have been following them for about two weeks or longer. My mom even said she has noticed how my attitude and confidence in myself have changed. The day I received your letter, I went right to my room and set some goals. Here are my goals for now: 1. Pray every night and day. 2. Pay my tithing. 3. Do not swear."

Her letter went on to explain some of her challenges, and again I wished that somehow she might have her burden lightened. During the following months other letters would come, reporting in detail past goals accomplished and new ones set. Over many months her goals evolved from the first steps in self-mastery to those which included regular scripture study, getting her family to attend church, and helping her father, whom she loved very deeply, with some of his problems. They included concern for her younger brother and sisters, an education for herself, and the ability to be self-reliant. She told of keeping a daily journal and recording her goals and her challenges, her discouragements, and her gradual progress. As she regularly marked off and recorded her progress, I was aware of her physical challenges (she had diabetes) in addition to other hurdles that continuously seemed to loom up in her way. I watched her strain and tire and be set back by having to repeat some classes at school, but she never gave up.

This spring I was invited to attend her graduation. As I watched the graduates walk across the stage to receive their diplomas, I wondered about the struggles and the challenges that could be told by each one who had mastered certain milestones and goals that were marked off in carefully measured steps until they were completed. Stretching to see around those in front of me, I caught sight of the girl with the long brown hair and the pretty face, which reflected greater confidence and assurance than before. It seemed appropriate that she was wearing a lovely blue dress. She took a step and hesitated. Then she walked confidently forward with the trace of a smile on her lips. She accepted her diploma with dignity and poise, not so much as one who is graduating, it seemed, but rather as one now victorious after a quiet inner battle, one who had broken barriers and was ready for new freedom. She had carried her own burden and could now lay it aside because of her own consistent, determined, unrelenting effort.

Something about that moment, like an echo from the past, took me back several years to a chicken hatchery in Hyrum, Utah. My thoughts went flashing back and forth, drawing comparisons and seeing parallels.

As an educational television teacher, I had arranged to do a program for third grade students to teach them how, after twenty-one days in an incubator, eggs are ready and little chickens hatch out according to schedule. It was this miracle of hatching out that I wanted to capture so that every child might experience the wonder and glory of the miracle of new life.

On the day that the chicks were scheduled to hatch, the television camera was set up and the lens was adjusted to allow for close observation. Then a drawerlike container, which had been filled twenty-one days before with eggs, was pulled out, and we saw many little chickens in different stages of development. Some that were ahead of the others were now free from their shells, and their downy feathers were dried and fluffy; others just out of the shell were still wet, with the down sticking to the delicate little bodies. We saw a little chicken using its tiny beak to break a hole in the shell that had encased it for twenty-one days. First just a tiny speck appeared; then gradually, little by little, the shell was broken away.

Curiously I picked up one of the eggs that showed no signs of life. I immediately experienced in the palm of my hand the sensation of constant movement within the egg. The shell that held the little chicken captive seemed like steel, to be able to withstand the great power and strength within. My desire to see through the shell mounted as the sensation of holding the egg captured my full attention. If the children could just see what was happening inside, they might be able to sense something of the miracle within.

Holding the egg close to the lens of the television camera, I asked Mr. Nyman, the owner of the hatchery, if I might use my fingernail to remove a bit of the shell very gently and carefully so I could reveal the efforts within and still leave the little chicken some of the struggle. Mr Nyman hesitated a moment and then agreed, explaining, "You realize, of course, that if you do, the chicken will probably die." The very thought stopped me immediately, and I placed the egg back in the drawer of the incubator. "Yes," he went on, "all the effort, the struggle, the activity that you feel going on inside that shell is a very necessary part of the little chicken's development. It is during this struggle that the muscles are developed, the respiratory system is strengthened, and all organs of the body are brought into use." I realized then that the help I wished to give the chick by removing the shell could actually cause its death. The process of hatching had to be contained within the shell, and only the environment could be controlled from without.

The miracle of life unfolding is the key to freedom. Once again the girl in the blue dress held my attention and I realized as never before that the load I would have lightened, the burden I might have carried, had it been possible, was the very ingredient needed for her freedom. Only by constant concern and careful attention to the outside environment can one help in the hatching, for the miracle of new life takes place from within. The struggles we would oft avoid are the very experiences that develop strength to endure a new environment.

She left the platform and walked down the aisle with her head held high, ready to safely endure and mature from the challenges awaiting her.